SCHOLASTIC

50 LITERACY HOURS FOR MORE ABLE LEARNERS

- Tricky topics covered
- Shared texts for a higher reading age
- Photocopiable activities

AGES 9-11

Helen Lane

CREDITS

Author
Helen Lane

Editor
Victoria Lee

Assistant Editor
Rachel Mackinnon

Series Designer
Anna Oliwa

Designer
Erik Ivens

Illustrations
Ray and Corrine Burrows

Designed using Adobe InDesign

Published by Scholastic Ltd
Villiers House
Clarendon Avenue
Leamington Spa
Warwickshire CV32 5PR

www.scholastic.co.uk

Printed by Bell & Bain Limited
1 2 3 4 5 6 7 8 9   6 7 8 9 0 1 2 3 4 5

ACKNOWLEDGEMENTS 

The publishers gratefully acknowledge permission to reproduce the following copyright material: **Jackie Andrews** for the use of 'Kidnapping of Sita' and 'Rama is Banished' retold by Jackie Andrews © 2006, Jackie Andrews, previously unpublished. **Anova Books** for the use of an extract from *War Boy – A Country Childhood* by Michael Foreman © 1989, Michael Foreman (1989, Pavilion). **Kevin Crossley-Holland** for the use of an extract from *Room for one more* by Kevin Crossley-Holland © 1998, Kevin Crossley-Holland (1998, Oxford University Press). **Eric Finney** for the use of 'Simple Seasons' by Eric Finney from *Another Third Poetry Book* compiled by John Foster © 1988, Eric Finney (1988, Oxford University Press). **Hachette Children's Books** for the use of an extract 'The brain' from *Look at your body – brain and nerves* by Steve Parker © 1998, Steve Parker (1998, Franklin Watts). **Her Majesty's Stationery Office** for the use of an extract from *What you need to know about driving licences* (D100) produced by the DVLA © 2005, Crown copyright and 'What is a visa?' from the Foreign and Commonwealth Office website http://www.ukvisas.gov.uk/. © 2005 Crown copyright material is reproduced with the permission of the Controller of HMSO and the Queen's Printer for Scotland. **David Higham Associates** for the use of an extract from *The BFG* by Roald Dahl © 1982, Roald Dahl (1982, Jonathan Cape and Penguin Books Limited). **Kingfisher Publications plc** for the use of an extract 'How you breathe' from *The Little Encyclopedia of the Human Body* by Richard Walker © 2001, Kingfisher Publications plc (2001, Kingfisher Publications plc). **The Newspaper** for the use of an extract 'Welsh star ready to shine' from *The Newspaper* www.thenewspaper.org.uk © 2005, The Newspaper (2005, www.thenewspaper.org.uk). **Jo Peters** for the use of 'Seasons' by Jo Peters from *The Works* chosen by Paul Cookson © 2000, Jo Peters (2000, Macmillan). **Peters, Fraser and Dunlop Group** for the use of 'The fight of the year' by Roger McGough from *Watchwords* by Roger McGough © 1969, Roger McGough (1969, Jonathan Cape). **Peters, Fraser and Dunlop Group** for the use of 'Reasons for seasons' by Benjamin Zephaniah from *We are Britain* by Benjamin Zephaniah © 2002, Benjamin Zephaniah (2002, Frances Lincoln). **Scholastic Children's Books** for the use of an extract from *My Story: The Blitz Diary of Edie Benson, London 1940-41* by Vince Cross © 2005, Vince Cross (2005, Scholastic Children's Books) All rights reserved. **Spike Milligan Productions Limited** for the use of 'On the Ning Nang Nong' by Spike Milligan from *Silly Verse for Kids* by Spike Milligan © 1968, Spike Milligan (1968, Penguin). **Usborne Publishing** for the use of an extract 'The Sun' from *The Little Usborne Encyclopedia of Space* by Paul Dowswell © 2001, Usborne Publishing (2001, Usborne Publishing). **Walker Books** for the use of an extract 'It's magic mould' from *The History News: Medicine* by Phil Gates © 1997, Phil Gates (1997, Walker Books).

Every effort has been made to trace copyright holders for the works reproduced in this book, and the publishers apologise for any inadvertent omissions.

British Library Cataloguing-in-Publication Data
A catalogue record for this book is available from the British Library.

ISBN 0-439-96563-2
ISBN 978-0439-96563-7

Contents

50 LITERACY HOURS
FOR MORE ABLE LEARNERS AGES 9 TO 11

This series of three books is designed to challenge and stimulate more able children. The activities in this book build on many of the key objectives in the National Literacy Strategy (NLS) at word, sentence and text level, across Years 5 and 6.

Each lesson is accompanied by photocopiable pages, designed to match the ability of more able learners. These photocopiable pages offer clearly defined, challenging objectives to advance children's practice in interpreting text in precise ways and communicating through writing with increased clarity. The lesson plans are designed to:

- enable teachers to retain and extend children's interest in and response to the written word
- build on children's knowledge and understanding of the written word to extend and hone their skills in interpreting text and in creative writing
- encourage more able children to maximise their achievement.

About the book

Each book consists of 50 lesson plans with accompanying photocopiable pages. In order to make the book easy to use, the lessons all follow a similar structure. The final lessons provide SATs style assessments in reading and writing along with guidance on specific target setting at this crucial time. At the back of the book are photocopiable text extracts chosen to reflect the text-level NLS objectives for nine- to eleven-year-olds. They provide prime examples of traditional and modern literature in a variety of styles and genres.

How to use this book

Each lesson is written to address specific NLS objectives from Years 5 and 6. These are given at the start of each lesson plan. The objectives grid at the beginning of the book provides at-a-glance details of the topics covered.

These lessons will help you to stretch children in imaginative and creative ways, often linked to other curriculum areas. They reinforce previous learning while offering children the opportunity to tighten and extend their skills in reading and writing. They are designed to stimulate and inspire children to recognise their own ability and achieve commensurate success.

Each activity provides a 'stand-alone' lesson that can be delivered as part of a wider teaching programme and is designed to fit into the individual teacher's planning for literacy. The lessons and accompanying photocopiable pages can be delivered by the teacher or a teaching assistant at any point in the school year although they also relate to specific term time objectives.

Title of lesson	Y5 Objectives	Y6 Objectives
Sets of synonyms	**T1. W7:** To explain the differences between synonyms. Collect, classify and order sets of words to identify shades of meaning.	
Idiom role-play	**T1. W9:** To collect and classify a range of idiomatic phrases, clichés and expressions. Compare, discuss, speculate about meanings and check in dictionaries; use in own writing. **T1. S7:** To understand how dialogue is set out.	
Text editors	**T1. S2:** To understand the basic conventions of standard English and consider when and why standard English is used. **T1. S3:** To discuss, proof-read and edit their own writing for clarity and correctness.	
Scientific bingo	**T2. W9:** To search for, collect, define and spell technical words derived from work in other subjects.	
Metaphor loop	**T2. W12:** To investigate metaphorical expressions and figures of speech from everyday life.	
Adding commas	**T2. S5:** To use punctuation effectively to signpost meaning in longer and more complex sentences.	
Variety of sentence structure	**T2. S8:** To construct sentences in different ways while retaining meaning.	
Prefix debate	**T3. W7:** To recognise the spelling and meaning of the prefixes: in-, im-, ir-, il-, pro-, sus-.	
Dictionary quiz	**T3. W12:** To use dictionaries efficiently to explore spellings, meanings, derivations.	
Prepositions word search	**T3. S3:** To search for, identify and classify a range of prepositions experiment with substituting different prepositions and their effect on meaning. Understand the term *preposition*.	
Origins of place names		**T1. W8:** To research the origins of proper names.
Etymological match		**T1. W10:** To understand the function of the etymological dictionary and use it to study words of interest and significance.
Active or passive?		**T1. S3:** To note and discuss how changes from active to passive affect the word order and sense of a sentence.
Proper punctuation		**T1. S6:** To secure knowledge and understanding of more sophisticated punctuation marks.
Proverbs		**T2. W6:** To collect and explain the meanings and origins of proverbs referring to dictionaries of proverbs and other reference source.
Understanding official language		**T2. S2:** To understand features of formal official language through collecting typical words and expressions. **T2. T17:** To read and understand examples of official language and its characteristic features.
Sentences for effect		**T2. S3:** To revise work on complex sentences: ways of connecting clauses; constructing complex sentences; appropriate use of punctuation. **T2. S4:** To revise work on contracting sentences: summary; note making; editing.
Reading arguments		**T2. W8:** To build a bank of useful terms and phrases for argument. **T2. T15:** To recognise how arguments are constructed to be effective. **T2. T16:** To identify the features of balanced written arguments.

NLS OBJECTIVES

Title of lesson	Y5 Objectives	Y6 Objectives
Crossword clues		**T3. W6:** To practise and extend vocabulary.
Word invention		**T3. W5:** To invent words using known roots, prefixes and suffixes.
Formal and informal dialogue	**S&L 49:** Listening – to identify some aspects of talk which vary between formal and informal occasions.	**T3 T16:** To identify the key features of impersonal formal language.
Dramatising complex issues	**T1. T5:** To understand dramatic conventions including how character can be communicated in words and gesture. **S&L 54:** Drama – to reflect on how working in role helps to explore complex issues.	
Constructing a balanced argument	**T3. T19:** To construct an argument to persuade others of a point of view and present to the group and present the case to the group and evaluate its effectiveness. **S&L 55:** To analyse the use of persuasive language. To present a spoken argument, sequencing points logically, defending views with evidence and making use of persuasive language.	
Note-taking at meetings	**T1. T26:** To make notes for different purposes. **T1. T27:** To use simple abbreviations in note-taking. **S&L 56:** Group discussion and interaction: to understand different ways to take the lead and support others in a group.	
Presenting a point of view	**T3. T18:** To write a commentary on an issue on paper, setting out and justifying a personal view.	**S&L 58:** To use a range of oral techniques to present a persuasive argument.
Dramatising emotional tension	**T2. T3:** To explore differences between oral and written storytelling.	**S&L 64:** Drama: to improvise using a range of drama strategies and conventions to explore themes such as hopes, fears, desires.
Book review	**T1. T10:** To evaluate a book by referring to details and examples in the text.	
Scene addition	**T1. T15:** To write new scenes or characters into a story, in the manner of the writer, maintaining consistency of character and style, using paragraphs to organise and develop detail.	
A writer's experience	**T1. T4:** To consider how texts can be rooted in the writer's experience.	
Formal recounts	**T1. T24:** To write recounts based on subject, topic or personal experience for (a) a close friend and (b) an unknown reader.	
Scientific explanations	**T2. T15:** To read a range of explanatory texts, investigating and noting features of impersonal style.	
Science research	**T2. T17:** To locate information confidently and efficiently through (i) using contents (ii) skimming (iii) scanning (iv) close reading (v) text-marking (vi) using ICT sources.	
Poster explanations	**T2. T22:** To plan, compose, edit and refine short non-chronological reports and explanatory texts, using reading as a source, focusing on clarity, conciseness and impersonal style.	
Historical point of view	**T3. T3:** To change point of view.	
Older literature	**T3. T6:** To explore the challenge and appeal of older literature through: listening to older literature being read aloud; discussing differences in language used.	

Title of lesson	Y5 Objectives	Y6 Objectives
Letters	**T3. T12:** To read and evaluate letters, intended to inform, protest, complain, persuade, considering (i) how they are set out (ii) how language is used.	
From story to stage		**T1. T9:** To prepare a short section of a story as a script.
Biography of a scientist		**T1. T14:** To develop the skills of biographical writing in role, adopting distinctive voices.
Nonsense poetry		**T2. T4:** To investigate humorous verse: how poets play with meanings; nonsense words and how meaning can be made of them; where the appeal lies. **T2. T9:** To increase familiarity with significant poets and writers of the past.
Challenging poetry		**T2. T6:** To read and interpret poems in which meanings are implied or multi-layered; to discuss, interpret challenging poems with others. **T2. T9:** To increase familiarity with significant poets and writers of the past.
Writing arguments		**T2. T18:** To construct effective arguments. **T2. T19:** To write a balanced report of a controversial issue.
Cyclic poetry		**T3. T2:** To discuss how linked poems relate to one another by themes, format and repetition. **T3. T3:** To describe and evaluate the style of an individual poet.
Season poems		**T3. T13:** To write a sequence of poems linked by theme or form.
Writing an extended story		**T3. T14:** To write an extended story, worked on over time on a theme identified in reading.
Reading test: Fiction	**T1. T9:** To develop an active attitude towards reading. **T3. T2:** To identify the point of view from which a story is told and how this affects the reader's response.	**T2. T8:** To analyse the success of texts and writers in evoking particular responses in the reader.
Reading test: Non-fiction		**T1. T13:** To secure understanding of the features of non-chronological reports. **T3. T17:** To appraise text quickly and effectively; to retrieve information from it; to find information quickly and evaluate its value.
Reading test: Poetry		**T2. T3:** To recognise how poets manipulate words for: their quality of sound; for multiple layers of meaning. **T2. T5:** To analyse how messages are conveyed in poetry. **T3. T4:** To comment critically on the overall impact of a poem, showing how language and themes have been developed.
Writing test: Shorter task (Web page)		**T3. S4:** To secure control of complex sentences, understanding how clauses can be manipulated to achieve different effects. **T3. T22:** To select the appropriate style and form to suit a specific purpose and audience, drawing on knowledge of different non-fiction text types.
Writing test: Longer task (School website)		**T3. S1:** To revise the language conventions and grammatical features of the different text types. **T3. S3:** To revise formal styles of writing. **T3. T22:** To select the appropriate style and form to suit a specific purpose and audience, drawing on knowledge of different non-fiction types.
Writing Test: Longer task (Letter)	**T3. T17:** To draft and write individual, group or class letters for real purposes. **T3. T19:** To construct an argument in note form or full text to persuade others of a point of view.	**T3. S1:** To revise the language conventions and grammatical features of the different types of text.

Sets of synonyms

Objective
Y5. T1. W7.
To explain the differences between synonyms, eg *angry, frustrated, upset*; collect, classify and order sets of words to identify shades of meaning.

Guided work

1. Before the lesson, ensure that each child has access to a dictionary and a thesaurus. Copy photocopiable page 9 so there is one per pair of children. Cut off the scales set down the left-hand side of the page, and join together the two lines marked zero. The children will use these scales (from -10 to +10) for grading synonyms.

2. Having checked that each child has a partner to work with, begin the lesson by asking the children for a definition for the word 'synonym'. Take suggestions and write them on the board. Agree that synonyms are words that have the same or similar meanings. Explain to the children that by using synonyms they can avoid overusing common words – and thus add variety to their writing. Ask the children to turn and tell their partner some words that might be overused (good, nice). Take feedback from the class on overused words and compile on the board a list of words to avoid.

3. Then ask the children for a definition of the word 'antonym'. Again compare and contrast responses and agree on the definition: an antonym is a word that means the opposite of another. Ask the children for antonyms of good (bad, terrible, awful), illustrating that a word may have more than one antonym.

Independent work

- Distribute copies of photocopiable page 9 and the separate scale. Explain that there are several sets of synonyms and antonyms on this sheet. Tell the children that it is their job to investigate the meanings of these words and then grade them on the scale according to their shades of meaning. For example, 'grotesque' may be placed at -10 with 'ugly' at -6 and 'plain' at -2.

- Ask the children to cut up the words and sort them into positives (for example, talented) and negatives (for example, hideous).

- Then ask the children to look for synonyms with shades of meaning that differ very slightly. Explain to the children that there are no right or wrong answers; each pair may come up with different results. The important thing is that they discuss this with their partner and justify their decisions.

Plenary

- End the lesson by grouping several pairs of children together and asking the groups to compare and discuss their scaling of the words. Prompt the children to look for similarities and differences and how these are explained. Finish with a whole-class discussion. Ask: Did anyone grade heroic as more positive than plucky? Why do we agree that ingenious is more positive than clever? Which are the most positive or negative words we looked at? Why were these words the most negative/positive?

Further challenge
- Set the children the challenge of finding further synonyms that could be added to each scale, encouraging the children in their use of the thesaurus. Where exceptionally unusual or creative vocabulary is discovered, allow the children to add their own words to the display, giving them ownership.

Sets of synonyms

0		10		chicken	talented	appalling	glamorous
–1		9		valiant	stupid	obnoxious	plain
–2		8		bold	dense	splendid	stunning
–3		7		intrepid	ingenious	impressive	hideous
–4		6		wimp	brilliant	upsetting	handsome
–5		5		plucky	intelligent	sensational	grotesque
–6		4		heroic	foolish	magnificent	gorgeous
–7		3		fearless	clever	repulsive	attractive
–8		2		courageous	dim	shocking	beautiful
–9		1		cowardly	wise	marvellous	ugly
–10							

Idiom role-play

Objectives

Y5. T1. W9.
To collect and classify a range of idiomatic phrases, clichés and expressions. Compare, discuss, speculate about meanings and check in dictionaries; use in own writing.

Y5. T1. S7.
To understand how dialogue is set out, eg on separate lines for alternate speakers in narrative, and the positioning of commas before speech marks.

Guided work

1. Before the lesson, copy and cut out one set of idiom cards from photocopiable page 11 per group; these can be laminated and kept as a permanent resource.

2. Explain to the children that as society changes, so does vocabulary. For example, the phrase 'surfing the web' is relatively new because the internet only came into common use in the 1990s.

3. Ensure that each child has a partner to work with. Ask the children to discuss with their partners what is meant by idiom/idiomatic phrase or cliché. Take feedback from the children; praise examples that illustrate correct use and write them on the board. Agree collectively that idioms are not meant literally but are understood by the people that use them. Explain to the children that idiomatic phrases cannot be inferred from understanding individual words (for example, 'under the weather').

4. Point out that an idiom becomes a cliché when it is perceived as being overused. Discuss examples of idioms and clichés that the children know. Compile a class list.

5. Join the pairs of children, creating small working groups of four. Give each group a set of the idiom cards and allow the children a few minutes to discuss them. Take questions about definitions and context. Then give the groups ten minutes to explore one of these expressions through role-play that puts the idiom into a context. (For example, a mother telling a friend that her child was under the weather with a sore throat.)

Independent work

- Explain to the children that their next task is to use idiomatic phrases in a written context.
- Review with the children the conventions for writing direct speech:

> - speech marks are used around the words spoken
> - punctuation is needed inside the speech marks as well as outside
> - a new line is needed for each new speaker.

- On the board, model an example of direct speech, verbalising thought processes as you write. For example: I shall begin the sentence with the speech, so I need speech marks and then a capital letter... ('She did well in her test,' said the teacher, 'so she was over the moon.')
- Explain to the children that they are to use their role-plays as inspiration for a short written dialogue that demonstrates the meaning of one or more of the idiom cards. As the children write, ensure that they use correct punctuation and layout.

Plenary

- End the lesson by allowing each group to perform one of their idiom role-plays to the rest of the class. Encourage the children to evaluate the clarity of the role-play and suggest improvements.

Further challenge

- Set a listening homework for the children. Ask them to listen to friends and family for more examples of these idiomatic phrases and clichés. Remind the children to listen carefully to the context and encourage them to ask when they do not understand.

Idiom role-play

beat about the bush	blow your own trumpet
getting off on the wrong foot	having cold feet
let the cat out of the bag	under the weather
given up the ghost	taken for a ride
past his prime	face the music
in for a penny	hit the nail on the head

Text editors

Objectives

Y5. T1. S2.
To understand the basic conventions of standard English and consider when and why standard English is used.

Y5. T1. S3.
To discuss, proof-read and edit their own writing for clarity and correctness, eg by creating more complex sentences, using a range of connectives, simplifying clumsy constructions.

Guided work

1. This lesson could follow an extended writing activity, enabling the children to improve their work.

2. Share with the children the lesson objectives, explaining that editing involves both improvement and correction. Distribute and read together the report on photocopiable page 13, written recently by a Year 5 child. Ask the children what improvements would make it more formal and well-written. Edit the text as a whole-class activity, while the children annotate their copies.

The improved text might read as follows:

> Coal mines were vital for survival during the Victorian era because technology and industry were developing using power from burning wood or coal. In coal mines there were three main jobs performed by children: trapper, hurrier and pusher.
>
> Children were hired to work down in the mine from the age of six years. On average they worked from five in the morning to approximately five in the afternoon, with Sundays as rest days. The workers received wages equivalent to ten pence per week.
>
> One of the three jobs performed by children would be that of a trapper. Trappers were mainly the smallest children because the passages inside the mine were only, on average, 26inches (65cm) high. Trappers were required to sit in the dark all day waiting until they heard the sound of a mine cart coming; on hearing a cart they would open the door to let it through.
>
> Alongside the role of trapper was the role of hurrier. The hurriers had to help load the mine carts. Once a mine cart was loaded the hurrier would put on a huge leather belt which had a chain attached to it. Once the belt was secure the hurrier would get down on his hands and knees and pull. This process could be repeated up to sixteen times a day.
>
> Occasionally hurriers would have a pusher to help with the cart. Pushers used their heads to push the carts when a hurrier was not strong enough to pull the cart independently. The pusher would be positioned at the rear of the cart.

Independent work

- Invite the children to add a concluding paragraph.

- Allow the children time to edit their own reports using the checklist at the foot of photocopiable page 13 – adding additional information in brackets, and/or using technical vocabulary.

Plenary

- Display a brief note written to the children by you/their teacher:

> deer children! just a short note to apologuise for my poor righting. I have been trying to make my righting better but am finding it harde. Do you think I need come extra lessons. From Mr Smith.

- Ask the children to edit and correct the note as you mark up the corrections on the board.

Further challenge

- Have the children write their own checklists before they begin a piece of writing. The checklist will provide a list of key features of a text and can be then used during the editing process. Keep checklists general and encourage the children to use them whenever they write.

Text editors

A report into the conditions for children working in a Victorian mine.

Coal mines were vital for survival at this stage because most things we used are powered either by burning wood or coal. In coal mines there are three main jobs hurrier pusher and trapper.

Children are hired to work down in the mine from the age of six years old. On average they work from five in the morning to aproxamately five in the afternoon also they have sundays off. The workers pick up about ten pence a week.

One of three jobs down a mine that would be available would be a trapper. Trappers are mainly small chidren because the doors are only 26 inches high. Trappers have to sit in the dark all day waiting until they hear the sound of a mine cart coming, then they open the door to let them come through.

Another Job is a hurrier. The hurriers have to help load the mine carts once one is loaded the hurrier puts on a huge leather belt wich has a chain attached to it. once the belt is on they have to get down onto their hands and knees and pull, they have to do this sixteen times a day. Some hurriers have a pusher to help.

Pushers are sometimes used to help hurriers. Pushers use their heads to push the carts when a hurrier is too weak. pushers push at the back of the cart.

Stephen Moore

Checklist for report writing

- Use descriptive language.
- Use technical vocabulary.
- Make generalisations.
- Use active and passive sentences.
- Be consistent in your use of tense.
- Write in the third person to make your report impersonal.
- Include background knowledge and factually accurate information.
- Use paragraphs.
- Include an introductory and concluding paragraph.
- Use a range of punctuation.

Scientific bingo

Objective
Y5. T2. W9.
To search for, collect, define and spell technical words derived from work in other subjects.

Guided work
1. Make an enlarged copy of photocopiable page 15, one per child.

2. Begin the lesson by asking the children for a couple of examples of technical vocabulary that they have used in recent science topics. Ask them to spell and define these terms. Ensure that the children's 'definitions' do not simply place the term within a sentence. Check in a scientific dictionary that the definitions given are accurate, and praise those that are. Begin a class list of technical vocabulary and meanings.

3. While writing your class list, ask the children to make up some sentences to show that they can use the words in context.

4. Give the children copies of bingo card A on photocopiable page 15 and explain that they will be making their own bingo game cards by writing in seven more definitions of technical words.

5. Distribute copies of the selection of scientific words from page 15. Select one word from those given and model for the class how you would go about writing a good definition. For example, orbit means: the path that one celestial body takes around another. Ask the children to provide examples of this word in context, for example: the Moon orbits Earth every 28 days; there are nine major planets that orbit the Sun, and so on. Note that the definition of orbit does not use the term 'orbit'.

Independent work
- Point out the definitions of 'solution' and 'evaporation' already written on bingo card A. Ask the children to select seven more words to define from the other suggested vocabulary on photocopiable page 15. They should write a definition of one of these words in each of the seven empty segments of their bingo card.

- Once all the children have a game card with nine complete definitions, begin a class game of 'Bingo' by selecting one technical term at a time to call.

- Ensure that 'evaporation' and 'solution' are called to correspond with the definitions already printed on bingo card A. Play initially for a row of three in any direction and provide a small prize. Provide a larger prize or incentive for the child who completes a 'full house' – crossing out all nine of their definitions.

Plenary
- Remind the children of the importance of the accurate use of scientific and other technical vocabulary. Ask some of the children to share their definitions and compare and contrast answers.

- Select a word not used in the 'Bingo' and ask for brief feedback on what the definition could be; accept as many answers as time will permit.

Further challenges
- Use bingo card B to play the game in reverse: the children write in the technical terms; you call out the definitions.
- Ask the children to provide vocabulary and definitions for words used in other subjects. For example, in ICT: a modem is a device that connects a computer to a telephone line, allowing transfer of data.

Scientific bingo

air resistance
amphibian
boiling
burning
cell
circuit
condensation
dissolving
electrical conductor
electrical insulator
evaporation
forces
freezing
friction
gas
gravity
incisor
invertebrate
irreversible change
liquid
mammal
melting
molar
newtons
opaque
orbit
pitch
reproduction
reptile
reversible change
seasons
skeleton
solid
soluble material
solution
sun
thermal conductor
thermal insulator
translucent
transparent
upthrust
vertebrate
vibration
volume

BINGO CARD A

The process of a liquid changing to a gas.		
		A liquid with a soluble material added.

BINGO CARD B

Metaphor loop

Objective
Y5. T2. W12.
To investigate metaphorical expressions and figures of speech from everyday life.

Guided work

1. Begin by introducing and defining a metaphor where something is described as if it were something else. Use the example: You are the light of my life. Ask the children to imagine what this would literally mean. Could a person be a light? What does the metaphor mean? Can the children think of a context within which this metaphor would be used? Then provide the children with the example: He had a heart of stone. Ask the children to describe this character in other ways. Can the children think of any fictional characters that would fit this metaphor? They may provide suggestions from literature such as Scrooge.

2. Ask the children to talk to a partner about metaphors that they have heard used in everyday speech. Take feedback on these metaphorical expressions, discussing the meaning of each in turn. The children may suggest metaphors from their own lives, such as: pull your socks up, learning times tables by heart and so on. Be aware that the children may confuse a metaphor with a simile. Ensure the children understand that a simile is a comparison of a subject to something else and often uses the words 'like' or 'as'.

3. More able children will appreciate the idiomatic nature of many similes (for example, as fit as a fiddle or as cool as a cucumber). Remind them that an idiom is a phrase that is not meant literally. Say that these idiomatic phrases cannot be inferred from understanding the individual words, for example: at a loose end.

4. Reiterate that idiomatic or metaphorical phrases are considered a cliché when they are seen as overused.

Independent work

- Cut out the cards on photocopiable page 17 as indicated. The cards can be laminated and kept as a permanent resource.

- Provide each pair with a set of the cards. Point out that each card has two halves. One half contains a metaphor and the other has a meaning: the metaphor and meaning do not match. Explain that the children must shuffle and deal the cards and then take turns to place a card on the table, matching a metaphor with a meaning, or vice versa: one half of the card put down should match one of the end cards already on the table – like dominoes. The first player to put all their cards down is the winner.

- Encourage the children in gaming strategies. For example, children should try to ensure their partner has to miss a turn. This can be achieved by placing cards down which the player knows their opponent cannot match (that is: cards in their own hand). Also allow the children to check meanings of metaphorical phrases in specialist dictionaries. Pairs who finish quickly should be encouraged to play the best of three games.

Plenary

- Invite the children to give feedback on any expression that they had not previously encountered, and to think of a context where they may now use this metaphor.

Further challenge

- Keep a bank of metaphorical phrases and idioms available for the children to add to their future writing and ask the children to investigate the origins of some of these expressions. For example, tenterhooks were right-angled hooks used to stretch cloth on a frame and the idea developed that a person's nerves could be similarly stretched.

Metaphor loop

Metaphor letting the cat out of the bag	**Meaning** raining heavily
Metaphor a wild goose chase	**Meaning** listening very carefully
Metaphor raining cats and dogs	**Meaning** in a state of nervous suspense
Metaphor keeping an ear to the ground	**Meaning** the final annoyance
Metaphor it goes against the grain	**Meaning** make more effort
Metaphor smell a rat	**Meaning** revealing the secret
Metaphor pull your socks up	**Meaning** it goes against what I believe
Metaphor sitting on the fence	**Meaning** pay attention to what I say
Metaphor she has butterflies in her tummy	**Meaning** have a suspicion
Metaphor pulling someone's leg	**Meaning** a hopeless undertaking
Metaphor mark my words	**Meaning** making fun of someone
Metaphor the last straw	**Meaning** she is anxious
Metaphor on tenterhooks	**Meaning** undecided
Metaphor to learn something by heart	**Meaning** pleased
Metaphor full of beans	**Meaning** to commit to memory
Metaphor tickled pink	**Meaning** in high spirits

Adding commas

Objective
Y5. T2. S5.
To use punctuation effectively to signpost meaning in longer and more complex sentences.

Guided work
1. Begin the lesson by discussing the purpose of the comma: a short break between different parts of a sentence. Remind the children that pairs of commas may be used as parentheses, identifying the subordinate clause.

2. Write this sentence on the board: Lunchtime was over, so the teacher explained the afternoon activities. Explain to the children that commas are used to separate clauses in longer and more complex sentences like this. Point out to the children that the main clause in this sentence is 'so the teacher explained the afternoon activities'. It is preceded by the subordinate clause 'lunchtime was over'. Explain that the comma aids the reader by placing a pause at that point in the sentence.

3. Provide another sentence as an example for the children: The children were very clever but they still struggled with exams. Read the sentence to the children and ask them if they can hear where the comma should be. (After the word 'clever'.) Give the children several other examples of complex sentences and ask them to place the comma. For each sentence, emphasise the short pause so that the children can hear how to read the punctuation. Examples of sentences could be as follows: Your homework was due in yesterday, but it hasn't appeared yet. Jupiter is the largest planet and Pluto, the smallest. My mother, who hated sport, refused to watch me play netball. Sarah loves pizza, chips and beans.

4. Discuss with the children the different purposes of the commas in the examples above: separating a list (Sarah loves pizza, chips and beans.); joining clauses (Your homework was due in yesterday, but it hasn't appeared yet.); avoiding repetition (Jupiter is the largest planet and Pluto, [is] the smallest [planet].); bracketing commas that come in pairs (My mother, who hated sport, refused to watch me play netball.).

Independent work
- Distribute photocopiable page 19. Point out that it contains no commas. It is the children's job to decide where all the missing commas should go, and to mark them on the page. Encourage the children to read the passage aloud to themselves, so that they can hear where the commas should be placed.

Plenary
- Make sure that each child has a partner to work with. Then ask them to read their passage aloud to their partner, ensuring that they read the punctuation accurately (with long pauses at full stops, shorter pauses at commas and so on).

- Read the passage as a whole group and ask the children to stand up each time they reach a point where they have inserted a comma. Discuss similarities and differences in the children's responses.

Further challenge
- Ask the children to investigate the use of the semi-colon and to find examples in their reading. Ask: What is the purpose of a semi-colon? (To separate phrases or clauses in a sentence; it is stronger than a comma, but not as strong as a full stop.) Invite the children to write their own examples of sentences requiring a semi-colon.

Adding commas

The Sun is at the centre of our Solar System and it is orbited by nine main planets and their satellites. From Earth the Sun and our Moon appear to be the same size but the Sun is approximately 400 times bigger in diameter than the Moon and nearly 400 times further away.

Every day the Sun appears to rise in the east and set in the west but in fact the Sun does not move in this way. Earth rotates on its axis once every 24 hours creating day and night. The rays of light travel from the sun in straight lines providing us with energy in the form of heat and light.

Although the Moon appears to shine it is not a light source. It actually reflects light from the Sun. The amount of light reflected by the Moon varies depending upon the position of the Moon in relation to the Sun and the Earth. From Earth the Moon appears to change shape depending upon how much light it reflects. We see either a full moon gibbous moon half-moon crescent moon or a new moon.

Sometimes the Sun Earth and Moon line up exactly so that the Moon casts a shadow on the Earth. This is known as a solar eclipse.

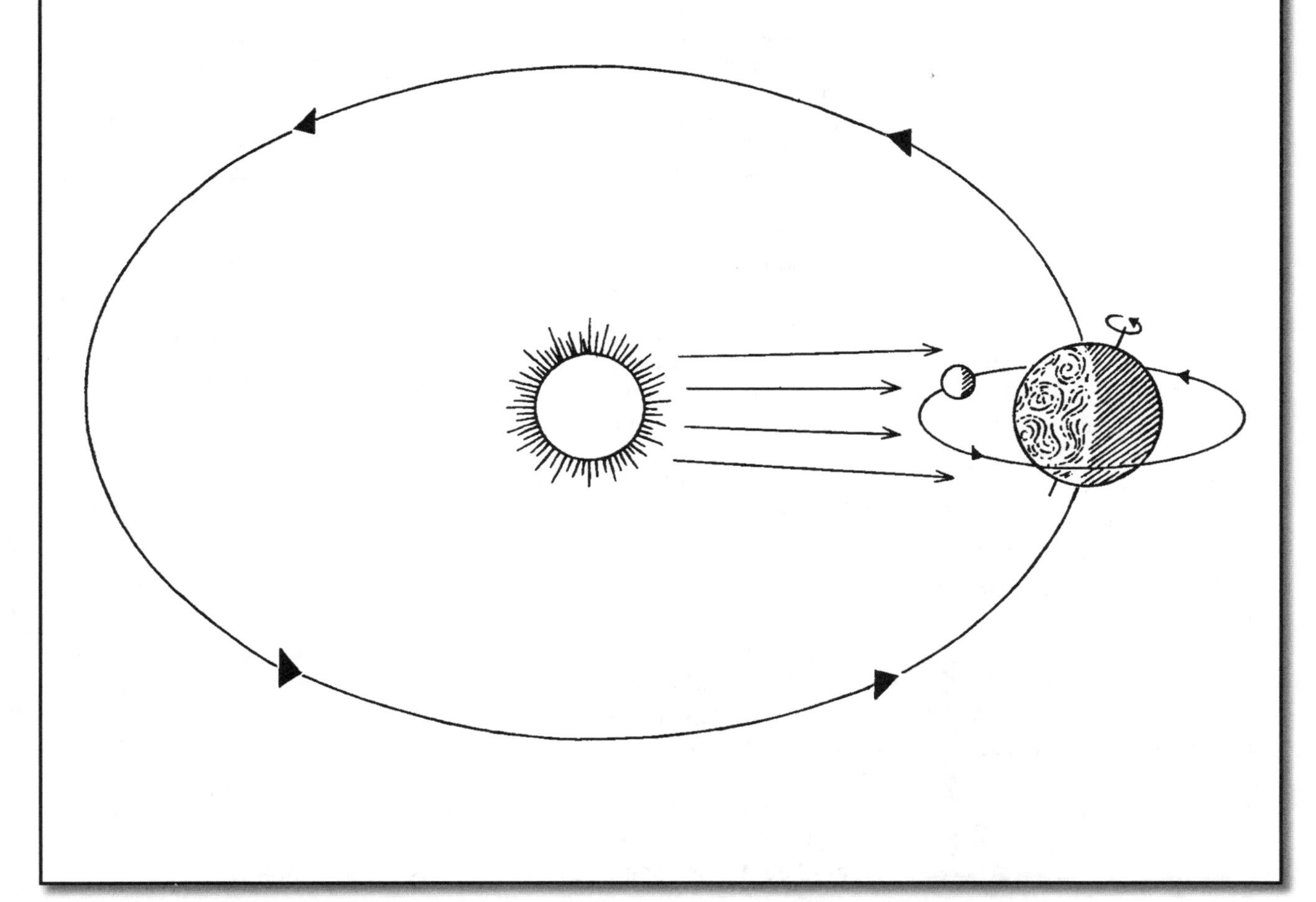

Variety of sentence structure

Objective
Y5. T2. S8.
To construct sentences in different ways, while retaining meaning, through: combining two or more sentences; reordering them; deleting or substituting words; writing them in more telegraphic ways.

Guided work

1. Before the lesson, split the children into four groups. Write in bold, clear writing, onto separate sheets of paper, a prompt for each group, as follows:

- Add more information, creating a longer sentence.
- Re-order the sentence so that it still makes sense.
- Improve the vocabulary.
- Delete some words from the sentence.

2. Begin the lesson by explaining to the children that they will be investigating and experimenting with sentences. Point out that every sentence can be written in a variety of ways, still making sense and still revealing the same information but in different and possibly more interesting ways.

3. Remind the children that as writers they should always consider how to make their work more interesting to read. Use the example: The teacher shouted at the children, as they were not listening. Explain that this sentence can be changed in several ways while retaining its meaning:

- It can be added to: The teacher shouted at the children, as they were not listening to the instructions she was giving them.
- It can be re-ordered: As they were not listening, the teacher shouted at the children.
- The vocabulary can be improved: The teacher bellowed at her pupils, as they refused to pay attention.
- Some of the words can be deleted to leave a brief statement in note form: Teacher shouted; children not listening.

Independent work

- Distribute copies of photocopiable page 21, plus one of the four prompts listed above. Allow the children ten minutes to alter a selection of the sentences according to the prompt given to them. Let the children self-select the sentences that they use to respond to each prompt. The children may ignore the fact that the sentences are numbered; for example, they may begin with sentence three if they choose.

- After ten minutes, move the prompts to different tables so that the children all have a different prompt. Time permitting, move the prompts again after a further ten minutes.

Plenary

- To end the lesson, take the sentences in order and ask the children to share with the whole class ways in which this sentence has been altered. Praise examples where the children have selected particularly adventurous vocabulary or where the word order works well. Look for children who split the main clause by dropping the subordinate clause in the middle, for example: The footballer, who was not selected for the team, was very angry. Explore with the children the shift in meaning created by the use or omission of commas in this sentence.

Further challenge
- Ask the children to select sentences from their own work (in English or in another subject, such as science) and improve upon some of them, using the methods discussed in this lesson. Encourage variety of sentence structure across all genres of writing.

Variety of sentence structure

1. The noisy children were asked to stay behind and finish their work.

____

2. As the postman delivered the post, the dog barked ferociously.

____

3. At the checkout several angry shoppers demanded refunds for the broken goods they had been sold. ______________________________

____

4. Sarah and Dominic fell out after she pinched his arm and called him names.

____

____

5. Sharon and Catherine loved to play skipping games in the playground.

____

6. Raj enjoys going to the cinema and seeing new films at the weekend.

____

7. Most children are scared on their first day at a new school, as they do not know what to expect. ______________________________

____

8. The roads in British towns become very congested in the rush hour as people travel to and from work. ______________________________

____

9. Spending hours on her mobile phone, Georgina had an enormous bill that she didn't think she could pay. ______________________________

____

10. The broken playground equipment was out of bounds and this upset the local children. ______________________________

____

Prefix debate

Objective

Y5. T3. W7.

To recognise the spelling and meaning of the prefixes: *in-, im-, ir-, il-, pro-, sus-.*

Guided work

1. Before the lesson ensure there are enough dictionaries or word lists for all the children to have one each.

2. Begin the lesson by recapping with the children on the meaning of prefix. (A prefix is a morpheme – the smallest unit of meaning – which is added to the beginning of a word to change its meaning.)

3. Review with the children prefixes that they have previously studied. (For example, auto-, tele-, mini-, anti-, mis- and so on.) Ask the children to provide as many examples as they can of words with these prefixes, encouraging them to explain the meaning of the prefix (auto: self; tele: distant; mini: small; anti: against; mis: wrong).

4. Tell the children that today they will investigate the prefixes: in-, im-, ir-, il-, pro- and sus-. Mind-map as many suggestions as the children can come up with of words that start with the prefix pro- (probable, proactive, propeller, proceed, prominent, projector). Discuss the meaning of these individual words, allowing the children to look them up in dictionaries if necessary. As the meaning of a word is discussed, make sure that the definition of the prefix becomes obvious, for example: a prominent scientist leads or is ahead of others in the field; a proactive person would be in favour of taking action. Allow the children to speculate on the meaning of pro- and agree that it means ahead or in favour of.

Independent work

- Write on the board the prefixes in-, im-, ir-, il- and sus-. Remind the children that they are to search for words beginning with these prefixes and explain that these will be negative words that could be used as insults. (For example, inactive, immature, irrational, illiterate, suspect.) Give the children ten minutes to find as many words as they can, using dictionaries and word lists .

- Next ask the children to speculate on the meaning of each of the prefixes they have investigated. Agree that in-, im-, ir-, and il- all mean not. Sus- is a version of sub- and means under.

Plenary

- Divide the class into two teams. Provide each team with a villainous character, either 'The Impossibeast' or 'The Unimaginadon'. Draw the characters on the board, or invite the children to do so. Ask the teams to insult their villainous character with the insults they have discovered. Allow the teams to 'throw' their best insults first, and praise new and exciting vocabulary. Score each team's insults, allowing one point per new insult and offering bonus points for innovative or spectacular vocabulary.

- Give the children a copy of photocopiable page 23 and ask them to consider what they have learned during the lesson.

Further challenge

- Ask the children to investigate other negative prefixes, such as: anti-, dis-, un- and de-. Set the challenge as homework and see who can come up with the longest word list. Encourage the children to keep a record of new and exciting vocabulary that they can use in their writing.

Prefix debate

My name is ______________________________

This is my assessment of the prefix debate that took place on ______________.

1. What is the purpose of a prefix?

____

____

2. Provide two examples of words that begin with each of the prefixes:

in- ____________ ____________

im- ____________ ____________

ir- ____________ ____________

il- ____________ ____________

pro- ____________ ____________

sus- ____________ ____________

3. What do the prefixes *in-*, *im-*, *ir-*, and *il-* have in common?

____

____

4. What does the prefix *pro-* mean? ______________________________

5. What does the prefix *sus-* mean? ______________________________

6. List and define below any new words that you have encountered today in the prefix debate.

Word	Definition

7. Many of the prefixes explored today have a negative definition. List below four more positive prefixes, with some example words. One has been done for you.

Positive prefix	Example words illustrating the positive meaning
pro-	proactive, proceed, progress

Dictionary quiz

Objective
Y5. T3. W12.
To use dictionaries efficiently to explore spellings, meanings, derivations, eg by using alphabetical order, abbreviations, definitions with understanding.

Guided work

1. The quiz on photocopiable page 25 will work with most Key Stage 2 dictionaries, but take time before the lesson to ensure that your dictionary includes all the words listed. Distribute the quiz (having first cut and folded them as indicated) and allow all the children access to copies of the same dictionary (otherwise their answers will differ).

2. Remind the children that a dictionary is a reference book containing words listed alphabetically, with their corresponding definitions. Ask the children to explain what other information might be included alongside each word. (The word type: noun, verb, and so on; the pronunciation.) Explain to the children that the word 'dictionary' comes from a 13th century medieval Latin adjective, dictionaries, which means 'of words'. Explain that the dictionary has evolved over the years. Show the children examples of specialist dictionaries (such as an etymological dictionary, a dictionary of grammatical terms or a thesaurus).

3. Explain that today the children will all be working from the same dictionary. Discuss some of its features, such as the guide to using the dictionary (usually located at the front of the book). As an example, ask the children to look up the word 'stick'. Discuss the definition. The children should have discovered that stick is a noun (as in a twig or branch or stick of rock). It is also a verb with several different meanings (ranging from affixing one item to another to persevering at a task).

Independent work

- Explain to the children that they are to work on the quiz sheet, page 25, in table groups (preferably four-person teams). Tell them that they can organise their groups themselves, as long as everyone is actively involved. Offer a small prize or some other incentive to the winning team.

- Give the children five minutes to complete each round of the quiz. At the end of each round, provide the children with the correct answers and respond to any queries. Rotate the answer sheets and allow each group to mark the answers given by another group. Keep a tally, on the board, of the number of correct answers each team has given. Between rounds, offer bonus points to the team that is ready first or recognises questions with more than one correct answer. (For example: tuck can be a verb, to tuck someone in, or a noun, a snack.)

Plenary

- Total the points and bonus points from each of the four rounds. Present prizes or certificates to the winning team. Remind the children of the importance of the dictionary for their own work, both for checking spelling and for developing vocabulary and understanding.

- Point out that many people, including staff at their school, frequently use dictionaries for reference.

Further challenge
- Set the children tasks and challenges involving specialist dictionaries, for example: to look up word origins in an etymological dictionary, to investigate curious phrases in a dictionary of clichés, or to write poetry using a rhyming dictionary.

Dictionary quiz

Round 1:

On which pages of your dictionary do you find the following words?

addition
computer
digital
football
millilitre
punctuation
rotate
skeleton
target
writing

Round 2:

What is the definition for the following words?

abdicate
choreographer
degenerate
fickle
incisor
obtuse
rhombus
sepal
translucent
unanimous

Round 3:

Which word follows each of these words in your dictionary?

athlete
conflict
either
harvest
longitude
novel
ratio
separate
thesaurus
weigh

Round 4:

What type of word is each of these words?

abide
callous
decency
eccentric
idiom
legible
lunar
perpendicular
so
tuck

Fold

Fold

Prepositions word search

Objective

Y5. T3. S3.

To search for, identify and classify a range of prepositions; experiment with substituting different prepositions and their effect on meaning. Understand and use the term *preposition.*

Guided work

1. Explain to the children that a preposition is usually a word that links a noun phrase within a sentence. It indicates time, position or direction, for example: We arrived home before dinner.

2. Tell the children that before is an example of a temporal (time-related) preposition and ask if they can think of any more.

Independent work

- Give the children copies of the word search on photocopiable page 27 and explain that there are 25 prepositions hidden within it. (For your reference, these are: up, down, in, out, on, under, over, after, with, at, by, except, without, beyond, against, into, between, along, across, behind, towards, since, throughout, before, during.)

- Tell the children that the words run both horizontally and vertically. Ask them to find as many as they can.

ANSWERS

o	u	t		a	t			a	f	t	e	r
n				l				c				
	b	e	y	o	n	d	u	r	i	n	g	
	e			n				o				
	t		a	g	a	i	n	s	t			
	w	t	o	w	a	r	d	s	i	n	c	e
	e	x	c	e	p	t			n			
b	e	f	o	r	e						u	p
y	n			o	v	e	r		w	i	n	
			d			b	e	h	i	n	d	
t	h	r	o	u	g	h	o	u	t	t	e	
			w						h	o	r	
			n	w	i	t	h	o	u	t		

Plenary

- Ask the children to classify the prepositions that they found in their word searches under the headings: Time (for example: before, after, throughout), Position (for example: under, over, behind) and Direction (for example: across, up, down). As they make their suggestions to the class, write them on the board under these three headings. Note that 'except' and 'without' do not fall into these categories. Can the children suggest a category title for these words? (Completeness, for example.)

- Then ask the children to think of example sentences showing how and when these prepositions would be used. Write some of the sentences on the board. Experiment with substituting some of the prepositions and discuss the effect this has on meaning.

Further challenge

- Ask the children to identify prepositional phrases in their reading and to keep a list of these to show you, for example: in the mud, by the chair, at the police station, before next Thursday and so on. Ensure that the children use prepositional phrases in their writing to answer questions using where and when.

Prepositions word search

o	u	t	q	a	t	r	s	a	f	t	e	r
n	a	s	d	l	f	g	h	c	j	k	l	z
g	b	e	y	o	n	d	u	r	i	n	g	f
c	e	v	b	n	n	m	q	o	w	e	r	t
b	t	o	a	g	a	i	n	s	t	r	s	a
c	w	t	o	w	a	r	d	s	i	n	c	e
v	e	x	c	e	p	t	t	y	n	v	u	q
b	e	f	o	r	e	o	n	m	n	b	u	p
y	n	c	v	o	v	e	r	r	w	i	n	t
v	b	i	d	u	y	b	e	h	i	n	d	t
t	h	r	o	u	g	h	o	u	t	t	e	d
y	a	e	w	r	t	u	c	v	h	o	r	b
h	f	g	n	w	i	t	h	o	u	t	v	c

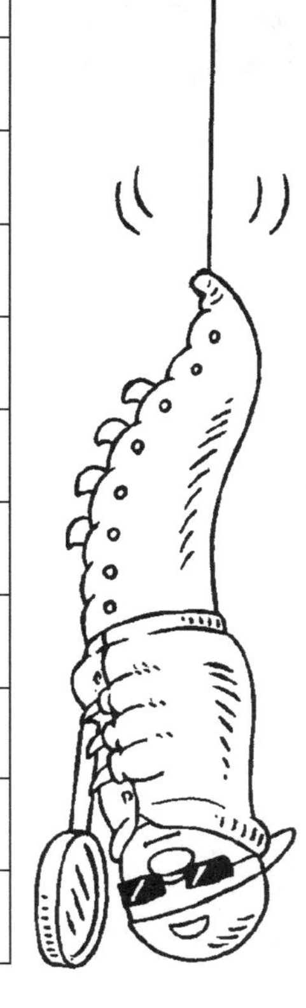

There are 25 prepositions hiding in this word search. How many can you find? List your prepositions here:

_____________ _____________ _____________ _____________ _____________

_____________ _____________ _____________ _____________ _____________

_____________ _____________ _____________ _____________ _____________

_____________ _____________ _____________ _____________ _____________

_____________ _____________ _____________ _____________ _____________

Origins of place names

Objective
Y6. T1. W8.
To research the origins of proper names, eg place names, surnames, the days of the week, months of the year, names of products.

Guided work
1. Begin the lesson by saying to the children that many place names mean something and provide information about the history of that locality. Explain to the children that in Great Britain there are Celtic, Roman, Saxon, Norman and Viking names. Make links to the children's history work on invaders and settlers.

2. Explain that many place names can be broken down, each part adding to the meaning. Give the children the example of Birmingham. This is an Anglo-Saxon name made from three parts. 'Ing' means people of that place, 'ham' means village or hamlet so 'Birm-ing-ham' means the village of the people of 'Birm'.

3. Ask the children for other examples of place names with the suffix -ham.

Independent work
- Give the children copies of photocopiable page 29. Ensure that the children also have access to atlases and maps.

- Ask the children to take each word part in turn and research what it may mean. Encourage them to look for clues by examining the physical geography of the locality, for example: evidence of a river at Oxford. They may also choose to use the internet for research purposes. Sites such as www.domesdaybook.co.uk/places.html list place names and their meanings.

3. When the children have finished their research, display an enlarged version of photocopiable page 29 and fill it in with the children (see correct answers and selected examples below).

Word or part of word	Historical origin	Meaning	Examples
tre	Celtic	village	Tregaron
porth	Celtic	harbour	Porthcawl
chester	Roman	camp or fort	Colchester
ton	Saxon	town	Leamington
ford	Saxon	river crossing	Oxford
dale	Viking	valley	Rochdale
scar	Viking	cliff	Scarborough
mond, mont	Norman	hill	Montrose
beau	Norman	beautiful	Beaumont
holm	Viking	small island	Holme
avon	Celtic	river	Stratford-upon-Avon
bourne	Saxon	stream	Ashbourne
aber	Celtic	estuary, stream	Aberystwyth
burn	Saxon	stream	Blackburn
thorp	Viking	daughter settlement	Scunthorpe

Plenary
- Ask the children to feedback to the group about places local to them. Encourage the children to apply the name origins to well-known cities, such as Manchester, Bradford and so on. Ask: What other common roots to place names could be investigated? Discuss the possible origins of the names of local places.

Further challenge
- Ask the children to investigate origins of other proper nouns. They may be particularly interested in researching famous brand names that they are interested in. For example: Coca-Cola (invented in 1886 by druggist Dr Pemberton; made from cocoa leaves and cola nuts), Cadburys (founded 1824 by John Cadbury in Birmingham), or Nike (founded 1972 takes its name from the Greek goddess of victory). The internet would facilitate this search.

Origins of place names

■ What do these prefixes and suffixes mean when used as components of place names?

Word or part of word	Historical origin	Meaning	Examples
tre			
porth			
chester			
ton			
ford			
dale			
scar			
mond, mont			
beau			
holm			
avon			
bourne			
aber			
burn			
thorp			

Etymological match

Objective
Y6. T1. W10.
To understand the function of the etymological dictionary, and use it to study words of interest and significance.

Guided work
1. Before the lesson, make sure that you have some etymological dictionaries available for the children to refer to. Cut out the cards on photocopiable page 31, enough for one complete set between two children. The cards can be laminated to create a permanent resource.

2. Explain to the children that they will be using etymological dictionaries. Ask the children if they have had prior experience of using these dictionaries. Ask: Do you know what you would find in an etymological dictionary? (An etymological dictionary provides information about the origin of words rather than simple definitions.) Remind the children that much of the English language is derived from Latin, French and the Germanic languages. Point out that the origins of more modern words can also be traced. For example, 'motel' is a portmanteau word, made by combining motor and hotel. A portmanteau combines words from different sources; can the children think of other examples? Brunch (breakfast and lunch) and smog (smoke and fog), for instance.

3. Reiterate that an etymological dictionary allows us to research the origins of words. For each word we can find out which language it originates from and which other words are linked to it. Use 'bicycle' as an example. Ask the children: Have you any ideas about the possible origin of this word? (Its origin is French, and it means two wheeled.)

4. Divide the children up into pairs and distribute an etymological dictionary to each pair. Invite the children to look up bicycle for more information about its origin. Further investigation will link bicycle with the Greek word *kúklos*, which means circle or wheel. The children will also discover that the word was first used in English in the late 1860s.

Independent work
- Provide each pair of children with a set of matching cards from photocopiable page 31. Explain to the children that the cards must be placed face down on the table, at random. They are to take it in turns to turn over two cards at a time. If they uncover a word and its matching origin they may keep the cards. If the two cards do not match they must replace the cards where they were, face down. Explain to the children that if they are unsure they will need to look the word up in an etymological dictionary to check the match. The winner is the person who has the most pairs correctly matched when all the cards have been taken.

Plenary
- Check the matches that the children have made; find out how many children won a game. Discuss the meanings and origins of the words. For example, ask: Were any of you surprised to learn that ketchup meant brine of fish?

Further challenge
- Give the children some blank cards and ask them to add more words with their origins to the game. Encourage the children to refer back to the dictionary when they learn new words.

Etymological match

bicycle 	From French (19th century) meaning *two wheeled.*
encyclopedia 	A medieval formation based on a Greek phrase meaning *general education.*
fame 	From French and Latin roots this word became popular in the 12th century and means *being talked about.*
grammar 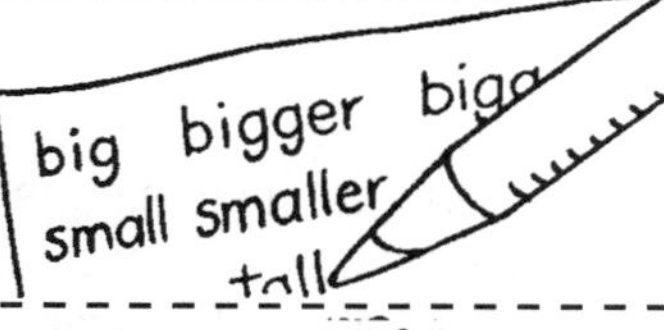	A word meaning *the art of letters* which has French, Latin and Greek roots.
grotto 	From a Greek word meaning *hidden place.*
harmony 	Comes from Old French, Latin and Greek and means *fitting things together.*
holiday 	This comes originally from the term meaning *religious festival* but was first used to signify *a day of no work* in the 14th century.
ketchup 	Originally a Chinese word meaning *brine of fish.*
lavatory 	From the English word root *lather* meaning *to wash.* This word means a place or vessel for washing.
parallel	This word has roots in Greek, Latin and French and means *beside each other.*

Active or passive?

Objective
Y6. T1. S3.
To note and discuss how changes from active to passive affect the word order and sense of a sentence.

Guided work

1. Remind the children that interesting writing includes a variety of different sentence types - both active and passive.

2. Explain that a verb is active when the subject of the verb is performing the action. For example: Steven broke the television. Steven is the subject and he is performing the action.

3. The opposite of this is the passive voice. A verb is passive when the action is being performed on the subject by someone else. For example: The television was broken by Steven. The television is now the subject of the sentence and the verb applies to it. Explain to the children that by using the passive voice they can keep the reader in suspense, for example: the door slammed shut, footsteps echoed up the corridor. The reader does not know who slammed the door or who the footsteps belong to.

Independent work

- Provide the children with a copy of photocopiable page 33 and explain to them that their job is to rewrite the disastrous day so that many of the incidents do not sound as if they are Helen's fault. Begin modelling this for the children, for example:

> The day began disastrously when Helen overslept, as the alarm had not been set accurately the evening before. Then, as breakfast was being prepared, the bottle of milk dropped and smashed all over the floor. While cleaning up the mess, Helen discovered that the tap had been left running and water was pouring all over the floor. It took half an hour to clean up the glass, milk and water so by this time she was running nearly one hour late.
>
> Eventually Helen was ready to leave the house. However, the house keys could not be found anywhere! Helen searched high and low but could not find where the keys had been left the evening before. After hunting everywhere, the keys were finally discovered in her jacket pocket and she raced to the bus stop. Then Helen discovered that there was no change in her purse to pay her bus fare so she was forced to walk the two miles to work.
>
> Upon arriving at work, Helen realised that her work from home had been forgotten - and she needed it that day. What were the children in her class to do instead? Could Helen's day get any worse?

Plenary

- Encourage the children to share, one sentence at a time, their alterations and editing. Ask: Does the new version make Helen sound more competent? Have you changed your writing so that you are not directly blaming Helen for everything that happened to her?

Further challenge
- Whenever the children read or write, ask them to look out for - and make good use of - passive sentences. Have a special pen or pencil available with which the children may highlight passive sentences.

Active or passive?

Helen's disastrous day

The day began disastrously when Helen overslept, as she had not set the alarm accurately the evening before. Then, as she was preparing breakfast, she managed to drop the bottle of milk and smashed it all over the floor. While cleaning up the mess, Helen discovered that she'd left the tap running and water was pouring all over the floor. It took half an hour for her to clean up the glass, milk and water so by this time she was running nearly one hour late.

Eventually Helen was ready to leave the house. However, she could not find the house keys anywhere! Helen searched high and low but could not find where she had left them the evening before. After hunting everywhere, she finally discovered the keys in her jacket pocket and she raced to the bus stop. Then Helen discovered that she had no change in her purse to pay her bus fare so she was forced to walk the two miles to work.

Upon arriving at work, Helen realised that she had forgotten to bring her work from home – and she needed it that day. What were the children in her class to do instead? Could Helen's day get any worse?

Proper punctuation

Objective

Y6. T1. S6.

To secure knowledge and understanding of more sophisticated punctuation marks: colon; semi-colon; parenthetic commas, dashes, brackets.

Guided work

1. Before the lesson, ensure you have one copy of the photocopiable extracts on page 120 and 126 for each child.

2. Read together 'The Mad Hatter's tea party' on page 120, which contains sophisticated use of punctuation. After a first read through, ask the children to try and read it aloud, ignoring all punctuation. (They will speed up and run out of breath.) Discuss how this demonstrates the importance of punctuation.

3. Begin to read the passage again, slowly. Pause at the end of the first sentence (beginning, There was a table set out...). This sentence is exceptionally complicated, containing four commas and a colon: it needs to be read carefully.

4. Discuss the purpose served by the colon (it provides more specific information about the general statement preceding it). Then ask the children to look at the commas, which serve different purposes. The commas surrounding 'fast asleep' are bracketing commas that work in the same way as brackets. The other two examples of commas serve to join the clauses and are both followed by the word 'and'.

5. Continue to read the text in short sections. 'Very uncomfortable for the Dormouse,' thought Alice; 'only, as it's asleep, I suppose it doesn't mind.' Review the use of speech marks around the text and corresponding punctuation. Look at the use of the semi-colon after 'thought Alice'. It denotes two sentences that are too closely linked in meaning to be separated by a full stop. Continue to discuss the punctuation in the text, including the exclamation marks, question marks and dashes (which demonstrate an interruption from the main sentence), and the use of quotation marks within speech marks.

Independent work

- Distribute copies of photocopiable extract page 126. Ask the children to annotate this piece of writing, commenting on the amount and type of punctuation used. For example: The opening sentence is an exclamation, the second sentence has two semi-colons that separate what could be three sentences that the author wants closely linked, and so on.

- Invite the children to use this text as a prompt for their own short story. Distribute copies of photocopiable page 35. Explain to the children that the purpose of their story is to show that they can use the whole range of punctuation shown on the sheet.

Plenary

- Invite the children to share their opening sentences with the class by writing them on the board. Discuss the use of more complex punctuation. For example: Is there another place in this sentence where the brackets could go? Does this sentence need a semi-colon or will a comma suffice?

Further challenge

- Ask the children to include all punctuation marks in the next piece of extended writing they do. Provide the punctuation marks and see how many they can include:
? , ! ... " " - ( ) : ; .

Proper punctuation

Are you using proper punctuation?

ABC	Capital letters are used for the beginning of a sentence and for proper nouns, such as Mrs Smith, London and Spain.
.	Full stops belong at the end of a sentence.
?	Can you use proper punctuation?
,	I like using exciting vocabulary, great punctuation and complex sentences in my writing.
!	Wow!
...	An ellipsis leaves you wondering what will happen next...
'	Apostrophes show possession, for example: Sarah's hat (the hat belonging to Sarah).
" "	"Speech marks are also called quotation marks!" said the teacher.
-	Hyphens separate within a word, short-sighted, for example.
–	Dashes separate words – before a list or when interrupting, for example.
:	A colon introduces the following: a list, a quotation or a second clause that expands or illustrates the first. For example: "We found the place easily: your directions were perfect."
;	A semi-colon is used to separate phrases which would make sense as sentences on their own; it is stronger than a comma, but not as strong as a full stop. A good example would be: Tolkien first published *The Lord of The Rings* in 1954; the film that was released in 2001 was a great success.

Proverbs

Objective
Y6. T2. W6.
To collect and explain the meanings and origins of proverbs, eg *a rolling stone gathers no moss, familiarity breeds contempt.* Referring to dictionaries of proverbs and other reference sources.

Guided work

1. Before the lesson, cut out the proverb prompt cards on photocopiable page 37, so that each group of children has one card. The cards could be laminated and kept as a permanent resource.

2. Explain to the children that this lesson will be about proverbs. Divide the class into pairs, asking each pair to discuss what a proverb is and to think of examples. Be prepared to provide examples if the children struggle, for instance: Make hay while the sun shines (meaning: Take advantage of favourable circumstances). Explain that proverbs are well-known sayings that enrich our language. They often contain a moral or warning; many originate from the Bible.

3. Write on the board the proverb 'Look before you leap'. Ask the children, in pairs, to explain its meaning. Encourage explanations that move away from the literal. Agree that it means: Be sure of what you are doing before you try anything drastic. Give the children examples of situations where this proverb might apply, for example: a businessman investigating an investment before he commits the money.

Independent work

- Divide the class into groups according to ability. Select one prompt card for each group, giving the most difficult proverbs to the most able children. Explain to the children that each group must prepare a short drama that will illustrate the meaning of their proverb.

- Use the example of 'The early bird catches the worm'. Ask the children to think of short sketches to illustrate their ideas on the meaning of this proverb. Praise those sketches that demonstrate an understanding of the proverb's principal message (act early if you wish to succeed).

- Allow the groups ten minutes to plan and practise their sketches on the proverbs assigned to them. Assist those groups that are struggling by providing contexts within which their proverb makes sense. Give each group the opportunity to share their sketch with the rest of the class. After each sketch, discuss how the drama has explained the meaning of the proverb and placed it within a context.

Plenary

- Explain to the children that these proverbs have their origins in British culture; people from other countries may not understand the metaphors on which they depend. Similarly other countries have proverbs based on aspects of their own culture. For example:

> - It is unwise to test the depth of the water with both legs. (Liberia)
> - If nothing touches the palm leaves they do not rustle. (Ghana)
> - When a lion cannot find the flesh to feed on, it has no choice but to eat the grass. (Malawi)
> - If you want to drink clear water from the well, be there first. (Zambia).

- Ask the children to match these proverbs to the English versions from the proverb prompt cards.

Further challenge
- Begin a class dictionary of proverbs and their meanings. Ask the children to contribute with examples they might hear at home. Contributions could be illustrated, as many proverbs conjure up wonderful imagery.

Proverbs

A stitch in time saves nine.

Many hands make light work.

Too many cooks spoil the broth.

The early bird catches the worm.

Let sleeping dogs lie.

There's no use crying over spilled milk.

There's no use keeping a dog and barking yourself.

You've made your bed – now lie in it!

Don't put all your eggs in one basket!

While the cat's away the mice will play.

Jack of all trades, master of none.

Beggars can't be choosers.

There's no smoke without fire.

Understanding official language

Objectives
Y6. T2. S2.
To understand features of formal official language through collecting typical words and expressions, eg '*those wishing to*'.

Y6. T2. T17.
To read and understand examples of official language and its characteristic features.

Guided work

1. Before the lesson, copy photocopiable extract pages 108 and 109 - one of each per child. Prepare an enlarged or overhead transparency version of each to facilitate group discussion.

2. Display the photocopiable extract on page 108 and read it aloud with the children. Then ask the children to define some of the more difficult words (eliminating or counterpart, for example).

3. Take each paragraph in turn and annotate it with the children, using photocopiable page 39 as a guide. Write notes on the enlarged text to guide the children through the annotation process. Re-read each paragraph in turn, identifying its purpose, along with examples of official phrases.

- The first paragraph is a general introduction that explains the purpose of photocards. It also explains who issues licences and why. Words such as 'eliminating' and 'ensuring' add formality.
- The two bullet points that follow explain exactly what constitutes a driving licence. Both points use formal vocabulary (endorsements, entitlement, application).
- The note in bold highlights the legal requirements and demonstrates to the reader the importance of both parts of the licence.
- The final paragraph explains how the DVLA will deal with licence renewal. Official phrases in this paragraph include 'validity period' and 'due for renewal'.

4. Encourage the children to annotate fully their own copies of the text. Their annotations should include definitions of unfamiliar words. Make sure you provide good quality dictionaries for reference.

Independent work

- Distribute copies of photocopiable extract page 109. Explain to the children that they must read and annotate this text independently, looking for the key features of an official text. (For example: formal vocabulary, impersonal voice and imperative verbs.) As part of the annotation process, ask the children to look up and define any unfamiliar words.

Plenary

- Discuss this second text with the children, listing on the board official words and phrases. (For example: entry clearance, entry clearance officer, British mission overseas, false information, immigration officer, circumstances have changed, validity of your visa, and so on.) Ensure that the children understand the meanings of all words and phrases listed.

- Summarise the meaning of the overall text for the children. (For example: People from some countries require a visa before they are allowed to enter the UK. The visa, or entry clearance, is placed on a passport and with this a person should be allowed to enter and leave the UK while the visa is valid. The visa tells officials in immigration why the person is travelling, how long they can stay and when their visa expires.)

Further challenge
- Ask the children to write an official text using the key words and phrases collected in this session. The subject of the text should be relevant to their own experience, for example: an explanation of regulations concerning the use of a bus pass, railcard or identity card, or instructions for completing a secondary school preference form.

Understanding official language

An extract from DVLA leaflet D100

Driver and Vehicle Licensing Agency (DVLA)

1. PHOTOCARD DRIVING LICENCES
DVLA now only issues photocard driving licences. This is to improve road safety by eliminating impersonation at driving tests and ensuring the person driving a vehicle is qualified to do so.

You will be issued with;

- a photocard; showing
  - the driver's photograph and signature which is electronically copied from the application form
  - categories of vehicles the driver is entitled to drive
- a paper counterpart document, showing
  - your signature (also electronically copied) details of any endorsements, and in the case of a
  - full licence holder, any provisional driving entitlement held.

Note: You must produce *both* the photocard and counterpart if requested by the police or a court. You should also present both parts when taking a driving test. You may also find that other organisations, such as car hire firms and insurance companies, will ask to see both parts.

Drivers will need to renew their photocard licence every ten years until age 70 to keep the photograph up-to-date. This will not affect the validity period of the entitlement shown on the licence. DVLA will send a reminder when the photograph is due for renewal. Drivers who are required to renew their licence at shorter intervals, for example, for medical reasons, or because they hold entitlement to drive buses or lorries, will not be required to renew their photograph at each renewal.

Annotations:

- Short simple sentence to introduce the overall topic.
- Formal vocabulary.
- Subject specific vocabulary.
- Bullet points used to highlight two main points.
- Imperative form.
- Subject specific vocabulary.
- Active sentence structure.
- Example of sentence in the conditional.
- Use of acronym.
- Formal vocabulary.
- Example of complex sentence where main clause is split by subordinate clause.

http://www.dvla.gov.uk/forms/pdf/D100.pdf

Sentences for effect

Objectives
Y6. T2. S3.
To revise work on complex sentences: ways of connecting clauses; constructing complex sentences; appropriate use of punctuation.

Y6. T2. S4.
To revise work on contracting sentences: summary; note making; editing.

Guided work

1. Before the lesson, take copies (one per child) of photocopiable extract page 112. Make one enlarged copy or overhead transparency.

2. Explain to the children that variety of sentence structure is vital in all types of writing. If applicable, remind them that in an earlier lesson you discussed using both active and passive sentences for variety (see page 32). In this lesson, you will explore using sentences of varied complexity.

3. Distribute the copies of photocopiable extract page 112 and display your enlarged version. Read the text together. Point out the long, complex and descriptive sentences that help the reader to imagine the scene. Note that a short simple sentence heightens suspense.

4. Write on the board a simple sentence: The teacher guided the children through the editing process. Ask the children how this simple sentence might be turned into a longer, more complex sentence. Suggest adding the information that the teacher was pleased with the children's efforts. Demonstrate three ways of extending the sentence:

- Pleased with their efforts, the teacher guided the children through the editing process.
- The teacher guided the children through the editing process; he was pleased with their efforts.
- The teacher, pleased with their efforts, guided the children through the editing process.

5. Point out that the initial sentence is the main clause. The extra information forms the subordinate clause, which may be added before or after the main clause, or may split the main clause in two. Ask the children to extend another sentence using this process.

6. Finally, remind the children that, while longer complex sentences add to the sophistication of a text, shorter sentences are still needed for effect and variety. Give the children the sentence: The lock in the door clicked and Susan found herself trapped in the dark passageway. This could be changed to: The lock clicked. Susan found herself trapped in the dark passageway – which heightens the tension.

Independent work

- Distribute photocopiable page 41, and read it with the children. Ask: Is this text well written? (No. All the sentences are of a similar length.)

- Ask the children to edit this piece, paying close attention to the variety of sentence structure. Suggest that the children select a few sentences to change so that the writing becomes more sophisticated.

Plenary

- Allow the children to share their edited passages with one another, initially in pairs. Read aloud and discuss some of the best. Praise well-constructed complex sentences, particularly where the subordinate clause splits the main clause.

Further challenge
- Ask the children to finish the story of Stuart (page 41). Encourage them to continue with the variety of sentence structure that they now have in their introduction.

Sentences for effect

■ Edit this text to provide a variety of sentence structure.

The school day had dragged on for ever. Stuart was bored of lessons and bored of his teachers. He longed to be outside on the playground. He longed to play football with his friends. He usually played football every lunchtime. Today though he had been kept inside to finish his work. Stupid maths; he didn't understand most of it anyway.

As Stuart daydreamed about the next match, he became aware of a presence beside him. Mr Taylor was standing over him. He was looking at his workbook. Mr Taylor sighed and muttered something under his breath. He walked away from Stuart shaking his head. Stuart wondered if he would be kept in to finish his work tomorrow lunchtime.

The bell finally rang and Stuart headed for the door of the classroom. From nowhere there was a booming voice behind him. "Stuart Daley, where do you think you are going?" It was Mr Taylor and he didn't sound happy.

Reading arguments

Objectives

Y6. T2. W8.
To build a bank of useful terms and phrases for argument.

Y6. T2. T15.
To recognise how arguments are constructed to be effective, through: the linking of points; the provision of persuasive examples and evidence; answering potential objections; appealing to the audience.

Y6. T2. T16.
To identify the features of balanced written arguments which: summarise different sides of an argument; clarify the strengths and weaknesses of different positions; signal personal opinion clearly.

Guided work

1. Before the lesson prepare one copy for each child of photocopiable page 43. Also make an enlarged copy or overhead transparency.

2. Begin the lesson by reading the text with the children and explain that this is a balanced argument. Annotate the passage together, labelling each paragraph:

- The first paragraph is the introductory paragraph, which sets the context.
- The second paragraph outlines arguments *for* the tests and explains these arguments.
- The third paragraph outlines arguments *against* SATs, with at least two different reasons mentioned.
- The final paragraph summarises and comes to a conclusion, in which the personal opinion of the writer is shared.

3. Next, point out the vocabulary within the argument, including the connectives. Highlight words, such as: vital, essential, furthermore, moreover; and phrases, such as: it has been argued that.

Independent work

- Ask the children to design a poster that will act as a prompt when they are writing balanced arguments in the future. Their poster may contain one or more of the following elements:

  - useful vocabulary, extracted from the text, for example: vital, indicates, problems, focus, aspects, and so on
  - useful connectives, such as: furthermore, moreover, in addition to, and so on
  - a writing frame, which outlines the basic content of each paragraph as discussed in the guided work
  - points to remember when writing an argument (for example: think of the feelings of the audience, express your own opinion, back arguments up with evidence, and so on).

- Remind the children that the purpose of a poster is to pass on information to a specific audience in an eye-catching and memorable way. The children will need to ensure that the key information in their poster can be read from a distance and that they keep the amount of text to a minimum, concentrating on key facts. As the children begin to design their posters, look for examples that have particularly good qualities (such as a memorable message or slogan, or a striking design) and share these with the group.

Plenary

- Put the posters up around the classroom and discuss each one in turn. Let the children evaluate each other's work. Ask: Which posters would you find most useful and why?

Further challenge

- Give the children a collection of newspapers and magazines and ask them to search for more words and phrases typical of a balanced argument. Encourage the children to use their prompt posters when writing a balanced argument.

Reading arguments

Should primary school children have to sit SATs tests?

Children in primary schools across England experience SATs tests at the end of Key Stage 1 and again at the end of Key Stage 2. At Key Stage 2 these tests results are collated by the Local Authorities and schools are placed in a league table depending upon their results. Position in the league table is said to indicate the quality of a school.

It has been argued that SATs are vital in measuring the progress children make as they pass through the education system. Furthermore they focus on the key skills areas of English and mathematics at Key Stage 1 and also include science at Key Stage 2: these areas are identified as essential throughout education. Moreover these tests provide parents with quantifiable information regarding the ability of their child, along with data regarding the quality of schools in their local area.

However, teachers, parents and pupils have campaigned for an end to SATs due to the problems that they cause. It is believed that the tests are an incredible strain on teachers and pupils, placing a huge emphasis on only two or three aspects of the National Curriculum and ignoring other subjects – particularly non-academic subjects, such as physical education (PE) or technology. Pupils feel under pressure to perform well and peer groups often add extra pressure to succeed. In addition to this, schools are unhappy with the league tables, which can label a school as underperforming when in fact the children have progressed well.

Overall, SATs are a stressful experience for all involved. They do, however, provide valuable data on attainment for both pupils and schools. If they can be administered in a "consequence free" environment, children will not feel under pressure to perform. It is possible that with proposed changes to SATs at Key Stage 1 there will be changes to follow for Key Stage 2 children.

Crossword clues

Objective
Y6. T3. W6.
To practise and extend vocabulary, eg through inventing word games such as puns, riddles, crosswords.

Guided work

1. Before the lesson, ensure that you have a variety of different dictionaries available for the children to use.

2. Begin the lesson by explaining to the children that they will be devising their own crosswords, which they will use to challenge one another's vocabulary. Use the example of the word 'audacious', asking the children to turn to the person they sit next to and explain the meaning of the word. Take feedback from the children and praise definitions that fully explain the meaning of the word. For example, audacious can be a positive word meaning daring or adventurous or it can be a negative word, meaning insolent or presumptuous. Ask the children to demonstrate their understanding of the word audacious by using it in a sentence. (For example: She came in, without being invited, and sat at the head of the table: how audacious of her!)

3. Ask the children how many of them have completed (or tried to complete) a crossword puzzle. Explain that a crossword is a series of interlocking words that are found by solving clues. Further explain to the children that they will be challenging their friends by providing definitions of words as crossword clues. Demonstrate on an enlarged version of the photocopiable page 45 by adding the definition for audacious as the clue for 3 across.

4. Ask the children to use their dictionaries to find a clue for 4 down; they are looking for a six-letter word that begins with the letter 'u'. For example the clue to relax or become less tense would lead to the word unwind. The clue parents' brothers would have the solution 'uncles'.

Independent work

- Hand out copies of photocopiable page 45, explaining to the children that they need to devise nine further clues, five down and four across, to fill up the crossword.

- Remind the children that the purpose of the lesson is to extend their vocabulary, so they should be looking for new and exciting words that will be useful to them in the future. Also remind the children that the words are all linked, therefore the first letter of 4 down must be the same as the fifth letter of 1 across.

- Encourage the children to work in pencil, so that they can make revisions as necessary. Also have some spare copies available.

Plenary

- Allow the children to test their crosswords on each other. Encourage them to work in ability pairs so that the most able challenge each other. To end the session, ask the children to share new and exciting vocabulary with the whole class.

Further challenge
- Display in the classroom any new and exciting vocabulary and encourage the children to use this new vocabulary in a variety of different contexts – for example, when writing stories, explanation texts or reading journals – as well as in their daily conversations.

Crossword clues

Can you complete the crossword?

Clues across

1. A seven-letter word meaning ______

3. A nine-letter word meaning ______

5. A seven-letter word meaning ______

6. A six-letter word meaning ______

8. A four-letter word meaning ______

Clues down

1. A nine-letter word meaning ______

2. A six-letter word meaning ______

4. A six-letter word meaning ______

7. A four-letter word meaning ______

9. A four-letter word meaning ______

Word invention

Objective
Y6. T3. W5.
To invent words using known roots, prefixes and suffixes, eg *vacca* + *phobe* = *someone who has a fear of cows.*

Guided work

1. Explain to the children that all words have to come from somewhere and that the words we use today come from a variety of sources. If applicable, remind the children of the lesson 'Origins of place names' (page 28).

2. Say to the children that languages from around the world have always influenced the English language. The children will be particularly familiar with this using the context of modern food: spaghetti (Italian), hamburgers (German), buffet (French), samosa (Indian) and barbecue (Spanish) are good examples. Prefixes, such as post- (for example, postscript) meaning 'after' and cent- (for example, centimetre) meaning 'hundred', come from Latin roots. The prefixes alpha- (alphabet) meaning 'a' and poly- (polygon) meaning 'many' come from Greek roots, while *nosthril* was the Anglo-Saxon word for nostril and *nosu* the word for nose.

3. Point out that new words are added to the dictionary each year as required by cultural changes and developments in technology. For example, the word 'mouse' now also means a device to operate a computer as well as a small mammal and the new term 'road-rage' means extreme anger caused by traffic or the manoeuvres of other drivers.

Independent work

- Cut photocopiable page 47 to make a set of cards (one per child), or ask the children to cut out the cards themselves.
- Tell the children that they are going to use the prefixes, suffixes and word roots shown on the cards to create ten to fifteen new words. Explain that to create new words they may add:
  - a prefix to a word root (for example, biomail)
  - a word root to a suffix (for example, mailphobe)
  - a prefix to a suffix (for example, photophone)
  - all three together (for example, microdictology).
- For each new word that the children create, they must also write a definition. For example, a 'mailphobe' is somebody afraid of communicating via the written word and 'microdictology' is the study of saying small things.

Plenary

- Ask the children to share some of their new words with the whole class. Write good examples on the board for discussion. Can the other children work out what the definitions would be from the make-up of these new words? For example, mediology could be the study of the media.

Further challenge
- Ask the children to research the meaning of the word roots, their country of origin and when they became part of the English language, using an etymological dictionary. For example: graph (meaning written) comes from the Latin *graphicus* (picturesque) and the Greek *graphikos* (of writing); graphic (meaning of drawing) dates from 1756.

Word invention

Prefixes	Word roots	Suffixes
anti-	dict	-phobe
micro-	graph	-ful
tele-	struct	-able
techno-	media	-er
multi-	camp	-phone
bio-	adapt	-tion
mega-	mail	-ology
post-	flex	-ive
photo-	ject	-ing
poly-	morph	-ness

Formal and informal dialogue

Objectives
Y6. T3. T16.
To identify the key features of impersonal formal language.

S&L 49.
Listening – to identify some aspects of talk which vary between formal and informal occasions eg contrasting excerpts from a national news broadcast and children's television.

Guided work

1. Before the lesson, record two examples of dialogue from television: one formal and one informal, and each lasting less than five minutes. (Ensure you are covered by an ERA licence before doing this recording. The informal dialogue could be taken from children's television or from pre-watershed programmes and may include some slang or regional dialect. The formal dialogue could be taken from an interview on the news or in a current affairs programme. Make sure that you can pause the clip for discussion during the guided session.

2. Show the children the two clips. Provide them with paper and pencils and ask them to record their observations, comparing and contrasting the two. Encourage the children to:

- listen to the way in which the two main speakers converse
- listen for the structure of the formal interview
- observe how the interviewer introduces the guest and how the interview is concluded
- identify particular features of the informal dialogue, such as regional dialect or slang
- make notes on examples of formal and informal uses of language in both dialogues.

3. Pause the clips at key moments, for example: after the introduction of the guest in the formal interview or after any slang or regional dialect in the informal example. Ask the children to repeat the language that they heard and classify it as formal or informal, explaining their choices.

Independent work

- Explain to the children that they will be conducting a formal interview with one of their classmates, using the formal interview as a model. Say that they must write out each question as fully and formally as they can. Provide the children with some examples of open questions that will allow their guest a chance to talk at length. (For example: Tell us about your family? Why did you choose to attend this school? What are your aspirations?) Point out that closed questions only evoke yes or no responses.

- Distribute photocopiable page 49. Ask the children, working in pairs, to write out fully the questions they want to ask. Allow the children to role-play the interview with their partner. Encourage the children to improvise around their questions, rather than sticking to a rigid script.

Plenary

- Invite the children to provide feedback on their formal interviews. Ask: Did it feel strange speaking to one another in such a formal way? Compare this to an informal setting. Ask: When are you likely to meet people in an informal setting and ask these kinds of questions? (When starting a new school, for example.)

Further challenge
- Allow the children to role-play different scenarios – either as an informal chat or as a formal interview. Link this to their current topic or science work by asking them to improvise an interview with, for example: Neil Armstrong, William Shakespeare, Louis Pasteur or Queen Victoria.

Formal and informal dialogue

A formal interview

Name of interviewer: ____________________ Name of guest: ____________________

■ Open the interview and greet your guest.

____

____

1. Begin with a question that asks about family background.

Question: ____

2. Then ask a question that asks about friendships.

Question: ____

3. Follow this with a question about academic likes and dislikes.

Question: ____

4. Then a question about hobbies or recreational activities.

Question: ____

5. Add another question of your own choice based on your knowledge of the guest.

Question: ____

6. Then a question about future goals or ambitions.

Question: ____

7. Finally ask a question about an inspirational person.

Question: ____

■ End the interview appropriately.

____

____

Dramatising complex issues

Objectives
Y5. T1. T5.
To understand dramatic conventions including how character can be communicated in words and gesture.

S&L 54.
Drama – to reflect on how working in role helps to explore complex issues eg sustaining work in role to explore issues from different social, cultural or historical perspectives.

Guided work

1. Before the lesson, prepare photocopiable page 51 as a series of prompt cards that will inspire the children's drama. Be aware that lessons such as this can encourage children to disclose information that they may otherwise not reveal. Also be aware of the child protection policy for the school or establishment within which you work.

2. Begin by explaining that during this lesson the children will be taking on the role of a variety of characters in a role-play exercise. In order to do this effectively, they will each have to understand the situation within which a character is placed and empathise with his or her feelings.

3. Discuss with the children the social and cultural context of your school and make contrasts with other schools in your area. Emphasise that your school is unique, for example: it may be in an inner-city area of high unemployment and may be multicultural in its make-up. Prepare the children for the possibility that the characters described in the role-play exercise may come from unfamiliar social or cultural situations.

Independent work

- Explain that you have a collection of prompt cards that describe the role-play characters. Each role-play is to be based on this description. Each child must imagine what life would be like for this character, thinking about how the person speaks and acts towards others and how he or she thinks and feels.

- Group the children in twos or threes, giving each group one prompt card. Explain to the children that they must devise a short role-play that offers insight into, and understanding of, this character's life. The character can feature in whatever scenario they choose and they can add any other characters they need. Give the children ten minutes to rehearse and develop their role-play. Encourage all participants to demonstrate to the audience, through the emotion in their voice and by means of their body language, their understanding of the character.

- Ask the groups to perform their role-plays, with the rest of the class as their audience. Allow the audience to question the main protagonists while the latter are still 'in role'. Praise responses that show empathy and understanding.

Plenary

- Invite the children to give feedback on how it felt to play these difficult (and possibly upsetting) roles. Help the children to understand that by taking on the role of the character they were made to think as that character. Through this, they may have gained greater insight.

- Discuss any stereotypes that emerged from the role-play. Do the children have fixed ideas about certain social groups or cultures? If so, offer exceptions and challenges to these stereotypes.

Further challenges
- Ask the children to write their own prompt cards for a future role-play activity.
- Encourage the children to empathise with other children experiencing difficulties, as reported on national and international news programmes (for example, children experiencing natural disasters such as floods or earthquakes, or children who may have witnessed violence or abuse).

Dramatising complex issues

Sarah is new at her school; she is very nervous. She doesn't think the children at her new school will be nice to her. She is very conscious of the braces on her teeth, and the children at her last school shouted rude names at her. Why should here be any different?

Michael doesn't want to go to school today. He hasn't been to school for nearly four weeks and he can't see the point now. His mum wants him to go, but when he shouts at her she cries and leaves him to stay in his bedroom.

Becky and Natalie have been buying cigarettes from the shop near school and encouraging the other children to try smoking. Leah has said no to them many times but they keep encouraging her just to try one. They have told her that she is being silly and immature by not trying a cigarette; Leah feels pressured to start smoking.

Jeremiah and his sister Aisha often come to school hungry. They lie to their friends about their home life; there is often no food in the cupboards. Today is the third time this week they have had no packed lunch.

Hassan is returning to school after spending the last four months visiting relatives in Pakistan. He is worried that the other children will have learned lots of new information and he will be left behind. Will he still have friends?

Felicity was involved in an accident when she was younger and now she cannot use her right arm or hand properly. She feels she cannot participate fully in school and she hates PE. She often tells her teacher she has forgotten her PE kit.

Luke is living with another set of foster carers, the fourth family he can remember. He doesn't care about school and is always being told that he is a naughty boy, even when things are not his fault. He thinks he has upset the new family he has been sent to live with.

Julie is moving house because her mum has a new job, far away. Julie loves her school and friends and she doesn't want to leave. She blames her mum for making her lose her friends.

Constructing a balanced argument

Objectives
Y5. T3. T19.
To construct an argument to persuade others of a point of view and present the case to the group and evaluate its effectiveness.

S&L 55.
To analyse the use of persuasive language, eg how a speaker uses emphasis, rhetoric and gesture effectively.
To present a spoken argument, sequencing points logically, defending views with evidence and making use of persuasive language.

Guided work
1. Before the lesson, find a map of the area around your school. Select two significant roads near the school that might be suitable targets for the fictitious traffic-calming proposal on which this lesson will be based. The proposal suggests that one of these roads should be closed to through traffic, perhaps with bollards at one end. The other road is to have speed ramps or sleeping policemen.

2. Begin the lesson by introducing the traffic-calming scheme to the children. Ask if they know of any points in favour of such a scheme. (Children who walk to school are sometimes in danger from speeding cars and the scheme might prevent accidents.) Begin to list these points on the board, under the heading FOR.

3. Then ask the children if they can see any potential problems with the scheme. (Local business may be affected because drivers choose faster routes and no longer pass their shops.) Begin to list these points on the board, under the heading AGAINST.

Independent work
- Explain to the children that the group is to be spilt: one side for and one side against the proposal. Assign the children to groups. Where possible, place the most able children in the group that contradicts their own opinion.

- Give the children photocopiable page 53 and explain that they should use this to plan a speech that puts forward the point of view assigned to them. Tell the children that their speech will be assessed separately from their written work; some children will have more confidence in front of an audience than others.

- Give the children ten to fifteen minutes to make notes and rehearse their individual speeches. Encourage them to pay particular attention to how they introduce themselves and their argument, and how they summarise and conclude. Tell the children that when assessing the presentation you will take into account their use of emphasis, rhetoric and gesture.

- When the children have had time to plan, invite them in turn to deliver their speeches to the class.

Plenary
- End the lesson by evaluating the effectiveness of the speeches. First, ask the whole class to vote on the traffic-calming proposal. Invite children who have changed their opinion to explain why.

- Ask the children to evaluate one another's public speaking skills. Ask: *Who do you think did well? What was persuasive about the speech?* Praise children who used emphasis, rhetoric and gesture effectively.

Further challenges
- Ask the children to write letters to the local MP or council – either calling for traffic-calming measures on a local road or asking for a policy change on another community issue.
- Hold debates exploring topical issues (for example, the introduction/abolition of school uniform or a ban on pupils bringing mobile phones to school).

Constructing a balanced argument

Proposal to be argued about:

Target audience:

Introduction
(State the purpose of the argument, grabbing the audience's attention.)

First argument
(Explain the main argument on one side of the debate and provide evidence and examples which support this argument.)

Second argument
(Explain another significant argument supporting the same side of the debate and provide evidence and examples which support this argument.)

Conclusion
(Restate the purpose of the argument and summarise the two main arguments – appeal directly to the audience.)

Note-taking at meetings

Objectives

Y5. T1. T26.
To make notes for different purposes.

Y5. T1. T27.
To use simple abbreviations in note-taking.

S&L 56.
Group discussion and interaction: to understand different ways to take the lead and support others in a group, eg identifying how to organise, chair, report, listen constructively and draw others in.

Guided work

1. Before the lesson, write on the board this short agenda for a meeting that addresses areas relevant to most primary children. Consider issues appropriate to your own school that may be discussed under 'Any other business'.

Agenda
1. Discipline and behaviour – small decline in standards: what can be done?
2. School dinners – are they healthy enough?
3. Playground equipment – is it adequate?
4. After school clubs – are there enough? Do we cater for all needs?
5. Any other business

2. Explain to the children that they will be holding small formal meetings to discuss these topical issues. They will each have a sheet of paper on which to record their notes of this meeting. All members of the group must participate in the discussion and all must listen actively to one another to ensure that accurate notes are made.

3. Say that meetings like this exist in a variety of everyday contexts, ranging from a school council meeting to a board meeting of a public limited company (plc). The purpose of a meeting is to discuss areas of concern or development and to decide on solutions or actions that can be taken. Tell the children that keeping records of such meetings is important as they tell us which actions were proposed, why, who agreed and disagreed, and so on.

4. Discuss with the children any previous experience they have of note-taking – from a non-fiction reading resource. For example, recap on the uses of shorthand when making notes. Provide the children with photocopiable page 55 and discuss the suggested shorthand. Point out that using acronyms (for example, AOB) is a type of shorthand and how other words can be shortened by selecting key letters (using chn for children, for example).

Independent work

- Organise the children into small groups of approximately five for the purposes of the meeting. Suggest to the children that they pause briefly after each item on their agenda so that they may update and clarify their notes. Remind the children that they cannot expect to write down all the dialogue: they must summarise, providing an overall gist of the meeting.

- Ask the children to begin their meetings. Ensure they follow the agenda. Praise those groups in which the children encourage participation of all members or show good active listening skills (looking at the speaker, nodding in agreement and so on).

Plenary

- Invite the children to reflect upon their meeting. Ask: Why might the minutes be vital later on? (Without them, people might forget, or disagree about, the decision made.) How did the children's shorthand differ? (Children may have different symbols for certain words.)

Further challenge

- Set up a class council and ask the children to nominate candidates for an election. Allow your council to meet on a regular basis and have class members taking the roles of chair, secretary and treasurer. Your class council can be given matters to discuss, including discipline issues to resolve or fundraising ideas to develop.

Note-taking at meetings

Meeting date: ________________ Meeting location: ________________

Present: ________________

1. Discipline (*dis*) and behaviour (*beh*) – small decline (↓) in standards: what can be done?

2. School (*sch*) dinners (*dnrs*) – are they healthy (*hlthy*) enough?

3. Playground (*PG*) equipment (*eqpmt*) – is it adequate for the children (*chn*)?

4. After school clubs (*ASCs*) – are there enough? Do we cater for all needs?

5. Any other business (*AOB*)?

■ Think of other ways of using signs and symbols in your shorthand. Here are some ideas:

☺ happy
< more than
> less than

@ at
♂ men/boys
♀ women/girls

∴ therefore
≠ not equal to
∵ because

Presenting a point of view

Objectives
Y5. T3. T18.
To write a commentary on an issue on paper, setting out and justifying a personal view.

S&L 58.
To use a range of oral techniques to present a persuasive argument, eg attracting and holding listeners' attention through what is said and how it is delivered.

Guided work

1. Before the lesson, enlarge photocopiable page 57 and cut out the separate statements. Display the statements all over the board, leaving room around them to write notes.

2. Begin the lesson by telling the children that they will be working independently, expressing their point of view and trying to persuade the other children in the class to agree; they do not need to consider the issue as a balanced argument (see page 52).

3. Tell the children that there are a variety of controversial issues displayed on the board. Explain that these issues are controversial because they evoke strong responses and opinions from people. Use the example: Children who wear hoodies are all vandals. Ask the children to indicate by putting their hand up if they own a hooded jacket or jumper. Does this make them vandals? Ask the children where this perception may have originated. Are there indeed some children who wear hoodies who are vandals? Is this an example of a stereotype?

Independent work

- Tell the children that their aim for the lesson should be to persuade others that their point of view on one of these controversial issues is the right one. They must express personal opinions and justify these with examples.

- Explain to the children that they will have 15 minutes of preparation time to decide how they wish to deliver their message and to plan the details of this message. Use examples provided by media advertising to illustrate persuasion. There will be certain catchphrases and jingles that the children are familiar with. Discuss the way those presenting these advertisements sound authoritative and how their messages remain memorable.

- Provide the children with scrap paper or planning books, encouraging them to persuade one another in any way they choose; more creative thinkers may choose to write a jingle, rap or poem to get their opinion across.

Plenary

- Provide the children with plenty of presentation time. After each presentation, allow time for reflection and evaluation. Was the message clear? Did it express personal opinions? Did it persuade anyone to change his or her own opinion? Was it an inventive or different approach? Do the children think the presentation was memorable?

Further challenge
- Ask the children to think of an issue regarding their own school or community on which they hold a strong view. For example, they may wish to campaign for a non-uniform day or extra playtime. Encourage the children to come up with a campaign strategy and then to present their persuasive argument to the relevant audience.

Presenting a point of view

Children who wear hoodies are all vandals.

All children who wear glasses are clever.

Religion causes war.

Schools in inner-city areas perform worse than those in the suburbs.

Teachers cannot follow fashions or trends.

Children who have no brothers and sisters are spoiled.

Boys are better at football than girls.

Children should be allowed to bring mobile phones to school.

Dogs should be banned from public parks.

All children should be made to complete homework.

Parents should be held responsible when children are late for school.

Video games cause children to be violent.

Dramatising emotional tension

Objectives

Y5. T2. T3.

To explore similarities and differences between oral and written story telling.

S&L 64.

Drama: to improvise using a range of drama strategies and conventions to explore themes such as hopes, fears, desires eg drawing on shared text to explore emotional tension at key moments in a story.

Guided work

1. Explain to the children that they will be:

- dramatising part of the Hindu story on which the Divali traditions are based
- exploring the hopes, fears and desires of the characters
- considering how a dramatisation of the story differs from the text version.

2. Distribute copies of photocopiable extract page 110. To set the scene, explain that King Dashrati had three wives, all of whom gave birth to sons. The heir to the throne, Rama, has married the beautiful princess Sita.

3. Read aloud to the children the story 'Rama is banished'. Stop occasionally to discuss the emotions of the characters. How does King Dashrati feel about banishing Rama? How does Queen Kaikeyi feel when she has persuaded the King to grant her wishes?

4. Tell the children how the story continues. When Rama is banished, his wife Sita and his brother Lakshman join him in the forest. Meanwhile his brother Bharata decides not to take the throne but to act as caretaker, awaiting Rama's return.

5. Distribute copies of photocopiable extract page 111 and continue with the shared reading of 'The kidnapping of Sita', inviting the children to discuss the emotional tension at key moments. How does Sita feel when she thinks Rama is hurt? Does Lakshman feel torn between Rama and Sita? How will Rama feel when he realises that Sita has been kidnapped?

Independent work

- Divide the class into small groups to re-enact the story. Check that the children are not over-reliant on the text - encourage improvisation.

- Ensure that the children are showing the emotions of the characters, both in their dialogue and in their reactions to others. Encourage the children to innovate and to use mime instead of props.

- Circulate among the groups, ensuring that all the children are involved.

- Allow the children to perform different aspects of the story for the class and to discuss the emotions demonstrated. Ask: How can the audience tell that Manthara is 'scheming' and the king is 'appalled'.

Plenary

- Compare the dramatic presentations with the original text version. Ask: What do we gain from these retellings? Do we gain a better sense of the emotions of the characters? Why?

- Distribute copies of photocopiable page 59. Ask the children to identify similarities and differences in the two presentations. Allow them to continue this activity for homework, to maximise research opportunities. Mark the children's work using the points scheme indicated on page 59.

Further challenge

- Ask the children to use the school or local library or the internet to find out how the story of Rama and Sita ends. Ask the children to explain why Divali is the festival of light.

Dramatising emotional tension

Comparing oral and written storytelling

■ Answer the following questions as fully as you can, on a separate piece of paper. The number of marks available for each question is shown in brackets.

1. Find three similarities between the written version of the story and the dramatised versions that were performed. (3)

2. Find three differences between the written version of the story and the dramatised versions that were performed. (3)

3. Which version of Rama and Sita did you prefer? Use examples to illustrate your answer. (2)

4. Find three examples of books that have been dramatised as films. (3)

5. Overall, do you prefer reading a text or watching the dramatised version? Explain your answer fully, using examples to illustrate your points. (3)

6. Think of two examples of oral storytelling other than film? (2)

7. Find the names of myths, legends and fables from other cultures that are more likely to have been passed on via oral storytelling. (3)

8. Use a variety of resources (internet, library, CD-ROM) to research the historical importance of oral storytelling. Summarise your research on a separate piece of paper. (5)

Book review

Objective
Y5. T1. T10.
To evaluate a book by referring to details and examples in the text.

Guided work

1. Before the lesson, collect a variety of book reviews, from different sources, for the children to read and discuss. The reviews should be of varied lengths and in different formats and they should review different genres.

2. Begin the lesson by explaining to the children that their task is to write a book review. Provide each table group with a selection of the reviews to read and discuss similarities. Confirm with the children the fact that none of the reviews disclose the ending of the book.

3. Provide each child with photocopiable page 61 and read together the publisher's press release, which provides information about the book *Storm Thief* by Chris Wooding. Explain that the purpose of a publisher's press release is to provide information about the book and to persuade people to buy it. A press release will describe all the good things about a book, whereas a review may mention some points about the book that the reader did not like.

4. Identify the genre of *Storm Thief* (adventure), the characters' names (Rail and Moa), the location for the story (Orokos), the enticing question that makes the reader want to rush out and buy the book (But have they discovered the key to unlocking the secrets of the city on the sea?) and the other information given, for example, the price and ISBN (which is generally above the barcode on the back cover of the book).

Independent work

- Explain to the children that they are to write a review or press release focusing on their favourite book, or one very familiar to them. Write on the board the following checklist. Your review or press release should include:

  - the title of the book
  - the name of the author and any relevant biographical information
  - the ISBN and price
  - the name of the publisher and a list of other books by the same author
  - the genre
  - details of how the story begins
  - a 'hook' to make the reader want to read the book
  - persuasive vocabulary (such as, stunningly, thrilling, provokes).

- Ask the children to write in the space provided on photocopiable page 61. Encourage them to use dictionaries and thesauruses to find exciting and persuasive vocabulary.

Plenary

- Ask the children to read out their reviews to the class. Praise each example that has a concise and interesting opening. Look for ways in which the children encourage the reader to read the book by asking questions or by implying mystery and suspense. www.scholastic.co.uk/zone/reading_reviews.htm has a selection of reviews written by young readers; children may be inspired to add their own reviews to this website.

Further challenge
- Encourage the children to set up their own book group, to meet at lunchtime or after school. Provide them with a suitable room and supervision. Provide sets of books for the children to read and discuss in this forum.

Book review

STORM THIEF

by Chris Wooding

In the midst of the ocean is the city of Orokos. No one can enter, and no one has ever left. At its heart stands the Fulcrum, source of the probability storms that change whatever they touch. When Rail and his friend Moa steal an unknown artefact they are forced to run for their lives. But have they discovered the key to unlocking the secrets of the city on the sea? Chris Wooding, winner of the Nestlé Smarties Silver award, has written a stunningly imagined, darkly thrilling novel for teenagers.

ISBN: 0 439 95957 8 Paperback £5.99

■ Write your own book review.

Title of book:
Author:
ISBN: Price:
Publisher:
Genre:

Describe the setting and characters:

Describe the build up of the story:

Persuade the reader to read the book:

Other books by the same author:

Scene addition

Objective
Y5. T1. T15.
To write new scenes or characters into a story, in the manner of the writer, maintaining consistency of character and style, using paragraphs to organise and develop detail.

Guided work

1. Before the lesson, make copies of the photocopiable extract on page 112 and photocopiable page 63, one of each per child. Also gather together a collection of Roald Dahl books.

2. Begin the lesson by discussing Roald Dahl's work. Encourage the children to tell the class about any of his work that they are familiar with. Ask the children if they have any favourite Roald Dahl stories or characters and investigate what makes them popular. Discuss features of his writing. Point out that many of the characters are vulnerable children or unsympathetic adults, as in *Matilda*, *James and the Giant Peach*, *The Witches* and *Charlie and the Chocolate Factory* (all Puffin Books). He appeals to the reader directly in the introductions to his books, particularly in *Matilda* and *The Twits*; he uses nonsense vocabulary which we understand, such as 'jumbly' and 'swallomp'.

3. Give each child a copy of the text, which is an extract from *The BFG*; many of the children will be familiar with this story. Read the text together, looking for common features of Roald Dahl's writing. For example: the way suspense is built with shorter sentences (Under the blanket, Sophie waited.); the use of description (her blood froze to ice) and so on.

Independent work

- Explain to the children that their task is to write about a character and a scene using similar writing techniques as those used by Roald Dahl when he wrote *The BFG*.

- Distribute photocopiable page 63, which provides prompts for the children to gather ideas for what happens in their scene, who the main characters are, examples of descriptive language, nonsense words to include and so on.

- Tell the children that they must write their scene, detailing what happens to the characters. Remind the children that they should organise their writing in paragraphs and that they must write using similar techniques to Roald Dahl. As the children work, read and edit their writing, looking in particular for use of paragraphs. Praise those children whose work reflects the original character of the writing and those who use nonsense words.

Plenary

- End the lesson by asking each child to read their partner's work and to identify in it the particular style features. Ask the children whether they have found a vulnerable child or an unsympathetic adult described in their partner's writing. Have any of the children used nonsense vocabulary? Are there any direct appeals to the reader?

Further challenge
- Play word games with the children, allowing them to invent nouns, verbs, adjectives and adverbs for use in their own writing. Encourage the children to base their words on known words from English or other languages, for example: *snozzcumber* (Roald Dahl's word for the foul tasting vegetable that the BFG eats).

Scene addition

- Use the boxes to record ideas for your scene.

Characters:

Summary of events:

Short sentences:

Descriptions:

Nonsense words:

Appeals to the reader:

Now write your scene. Continue on another sheet of paper if you need to.

____

____

____

____

____

____

A writer's experience

Objective

Y5. T1. T4.

To consider how texts can be rooted in the writer's experience, eg historical events and places, experience of wartime, friendship, holidays.

Guided work

1. Write on the board some key facts about the Second World War, encouraging the children to contribute. (The war started in 1939; Jewish people were persecuted; Adolf Hitler was the leader of the Nazi party in Germany and so on.) Refer to other world events that the children have learned about.

3. Tell the children that they will be reading two texts rooted in the writers' wartime experience. Distribute the photocopiable extracts on pages 113 and 114 and ask the children to read both – annotating them with comments on similarities and differences.

4. Ask the children: What are the similarities between the two texts? (Both are rooted in the writer's childhood experience and are therefore autobiographical; both focus on the Second World War; both introduce family members and their characteristics; both reveal the emotional state of the writer.) Then discuss differences between the texts. ('Blackout' is taken from a diary by Edie Benson: it feels more immediate, as if events are 'happening now' and includes examples of slang: Jerry's used for German's; and idiomatic expressions: off his rocker; 'Air Raid' is based on recollections of a time long past.)

5. Discuss the characters in the extracts. List them on the board, with key facts about each. What do the children already know about them? Is Edie scared by the blackout? How do the members of her family interact?

Independent work

- Ask the children to select one character and imagine what it would be like for this person to experience the events described.

- Use the example of Edie Benson (Friday 2 August 1940), describing the arrival of the policeman. How would Edie have felt? How would she explain this event to a close friend? What would Edie have been thinking as she overheard the fuss downstairs?

- Explain to the children that this event is described from Edie's perspective only. How might her sister Shirl have perceived the event? Would she have felt scared as the policeman burst into their bedroom?

- Provide the children with photocopiable page 65. Organise the children into small groups and ask them to take turns to play the part of a character and be in the 'hot seat'. The others in the group are to select questions to ask the character, from page 65. Time each interview using a stopwatch. Invite a new child to the hot seat every four minutes.

Plenary

- Ask the children why these two books were published. What do we gain from reading them? (They enable us to understand the experiences of the authors and to empathise with their feelings. They also raise awareness of important historical events, ensuring that they are not forgotten.)

Further challenge

- Extend this activity by asking the children to write diary entries for the other characters: for example, Shirl (Edie's sister with whom she shared a bedroom) or Ivan (the war boy's brother). Ensure that the children achieve consistency with the original text, particularly in any descriptions of specific events.

A writer's experience

- Choose from the questions below to ask the character in the 'hot seat'.

What happened before this event?

Who in your family do you get along with the most?

What happened after the event?

How did this make you feel?

What makes you feel frightened?

What do you hope for yourself for the future?

What do you enjoy doing in your free time?

What makes you angry?

What do you dream about?

When was the last time you felt really happy and why?

What do you think will happen to you tomorrow?

Who in your family are you most like?

Formal recounts

Objective
Y5. T1. T24.
To write recounts based on subject, topic or personal experience for (a) a close friend and (b) an unknown reader, eg an account of a match, a historical event.

Guided work

1. Before the lesson, make copies of photocopiable extract page 115 and photocopiable page 67 (one per child).

2. Begin the lesson by introducing to the children the life and work of Alexander Fleming, who discovered penicillin in 1928. Ask: Have you heard of this scientist? Can you name other scientific discoveries? (1796, Edward Jenner's smallpox vaccination; 1846, William Morton's anaesthetic; 1861, Louis Pasteur's link between micro-organisms and disease; 1865, Joseph Lister's antiseptic; 1895, Wilhelm Roentgen's X-ray machine.)

3. Put the discovery of penicillin into context by linking it to the science curriculum on micro-organisms and 'developing knowledge and understanding of famous scientists and their discoveries' (SC1 focus).

4. Distribute copies of photocopiable extract page 115 and read it together. Discuss: the technical language (laboratory, bacteria, disinfect); the formal phrasing (pressing work, extracted, the development of); the use of the first person.

5. Discuss with the children the event itself. Having checked that they understand the meaning of the word 'empathise' (using one's imagination to understand how another person might feel), ask them to empathise with Alexander Fleming. How would he have felt on discovering the mould had killed off the bacteria? How would he have felt when he realised that he could not develop penicillin immediately? Ask: Do any of you hope to become scientists?

Independent work

- Explain to the children that they will be taking on the role of Alexander Fleming, empathising with him throughout his research. They will be writing a letter from Fleming to a close friend. Remind the children of: the layout needed for a letter, the use of personal pronouns, reference to emotions, use of colloquialisms and so on. Also remind them that, despite the informal nature of the letter, the description of events must remain accurate. The date should be circa 1928.

- As the children write, encourage them to read, edit and revise their work. Allow them five minutes to work in pairs on editing their work. Encourage them to look for specific examples of the criteria outlined earlier. Ask: Did you include emotions, colloquialisms and personal pronouns?

Plenary

- End the lesson by asking one of the children to take on the role of Alexander Fleming for a formal interview. Ask the rest of the group to think of questions that can be put to your very own Alexander Fleming and encourage comprehensive answers that include factually accurate information.

Further challenge
- Give the children copies of photocopiable page 67 and ask the children to write their own newspaper report on the discovery of penicillin. Unlike the article on page 115, this report must be written as if for a newspaper: it should use third person narrative, formal and scientific vocabulary, impersonal pronouns, a headline, subheadings and accurate detail.

Formal recounts

The Daily Discovery

Tuesday, 4th September 1928

IT'S MOULD MAGIC!

Scottish doctor Alexander Fleming amazed the world yesterday with a discovery that could save lives. The doctor, who made his discovery in a sink full of dirty dishes gathering mould, believes that his find will revolutionise the way we treat disease.

Main article

Concluding statement

Picture

Caption

Scientific explanations

Objective
Y5. T2. T15.
To read a range of explanatory texts, investigating and noting features of impersonal style, eg complex sentences: use of passive voice; technical vocabulary; hypothetical language.

Guided work

1. Before the lesson, make copies of photocopiable extract pages 116, 117 and 118 and photocopiable page 69 (one of each per child). Make enlargements or overhead transparencies (OHTs) of all three texts.

2. Display the photocopiable extract ('The brain'). Ask: What type of text is this? (An explanatory text.) Read the text together and discuss the scientific facts (for example, the brain weighs one-fiftieth of body weight).

3. Point out key features of a non-fiction text: the subheading (Blood to the brain) and the diagrams (the diagram of the different regions of the brain). Ask: Why is the text set out like this? (The layout facilitates quick information retrieval.) Annotate the enlarged copy or OHT.

4. Next, pick out features of an explanatory text: impersonal style (The human brain fills the top half of the head.); technical vocabulary (cerebrum, lobe, hemispheres); generalised statements (Inside the brain lie the parts that are involved with your emotions and the automatic running of your body); passive voice (damage can also be caused by a blocked blood vessel). Remind the children that the passive does not reveal the motivator behind the verb (we do not know what is blocking the blood vessel). Ask: Can you identify other passive statements or formal phrasing? Allow the children to annotate the text.

5. Read photocopiable extract page 117 ('The Sun') - another explanatory text. Ask the children to identify key features as you annotate it. (Technical vocabulary, the passive voice, and generalisations and hypothetical questions - which are there to interest the reader, but do not affect outcome.)

Independent work

- Distribute copies of photocopiable extract page 118 ('How you breathe') and photocopiable page 69. Ask the children to read the text and identify the features listed. Use examples from 'The brain' and 'The Sun' to remind them about these features and their contribution to the text.

Plenary

- Review in turn the different features of an explanatory text. Ask the children for examples from 'How you breathe'.

- Responses may include: technical or scientific vocabulary; formal phrasing; complex sentences; the passive voice; generalisations; diagrams. Allow the children to mark their own work. Praise those who have found several examples of each feature.

- Ask: Can you think of a hypothetical question to add to the text? (For example: Have you ever considered why tiny hairs grow in our nostrils?)

- Collect and keep the copies of photocopiable extract pages 116, 117, and 118, if possible, for use in future lessons (for example, 'Poster explanations' on page 72).

Further challenge
- Display on the wall the key features of an explanatory text. Encourage the children to read other explanatory texts and recognise these features - technical vocabulary and use of the passive voice in particular.

Scientific explanations

■ Locate and write down examples of the following features within the explanatory text:

Technical or scientific vocabulary ______________________________

____

____

____

Formal phrasing ______________________________

____

____

Complex sentences ______________________________

____

____

The passive voice ______________________________

____

____

Generalisations ______________________________

____

____

Information passed on in diagrammatical form ______________________________

____

____

____

Science research

Objective

Y5. T2. T17.

To locate information confidently and efficiently through (i) using contents (ii) skimming to gain overall sense of the text (iii) scanning to locate specific information (iv) close reading to aid understanding (v) text-marking (vi) using ICT sources.

Guided work

1. Before the lesson, make copies of photocopiable extract page 117 and photocopiable page 71 (one of each per child). Check the websites of your choice and ensure that all ICT equipment is ready, together with some science books, encyclopedias and/or CD-ROMs. You will need a stopwatch to time the 'Independent work' session (see below), a list of correct answers to the questions on page 71 and small prizes for the children who perform the best.

2. Begin the lesson by reminding the children that different types of text can be approached in different ways. For example, a narrative would be read from beginning to end to gain a full sense of the structure, plot and characters. A non-fiction text could be skimmed, if the reader were looking for specific information.

3. Tell the children that in this lesson they will be locating information in non-fiction texts by skimming, scanning and close reading, and by using ICT. Advise the children to initially skim over non-fiction texts, taking into account the layout and any changes in format or text type.

4. Use the photocopiable extract on page 118 as an example, pointing out that, by skimming over the text they can extract key facts (for example, the temperature on the surface of the Sun). Where possible, encourage the children to text-mark, highlighting key words, phrases and facts so that they are easily relocated. When working with ICT sources (websites or CD-ROMs) they could print out pages as necessary and text-mark those.

Independent work

- Distribute copies of photocopiable page 71. Tell the children that the ten questions all have specific answers. In order to find these, the children will need to research a variety of sources, using indexes and contents listings to quickly and efficiently locate the necessary facts. Say to the children that they have access to certain websites, of your choice. They can also use encyclopedias and science reference books, if they prefer.

- Provide healthy competition for the children by offering an incentive for the child with the most correct answers or the child who finishes in the quickest time. Have a stopwatch available to add motivation and pace to this activity. Praise children who work independently and have the confidence to tackle this alone.

Plenary

- Review with the children the answers to the quiz, providing instant feedback. With each response, discuss where the answers were discovered. Did children prefer using the internet, CD-ROMs or books? Provide small prizes (stickers, team points, pencils) to the children obtaining the most correct answers in the shortest time.

Further challenge

- Ask the children to write their own quiz questions for one another, using the same research tools. Encourage the children to provide challenging yet realistic questions for their peers and use these in a class quiz.

Science research

How quickly and efficiently can you locate the answers to these questions? Work as independently as you can.

1. What is the distance from the Earth to the Sun? ______
2. Name a fossil fuel and describe how it is formed.
______
______
3. How does milk become cheese?
______
______
4. What is the chemical formula for salt? ______
5. Who discovered penicillin and when? ______
6. What is the *corpus callosum* and what does it do?
______
______
7. When was Marie Curie investigating radioactive decay? ______
8. What is the function of the alveoli in the lung?
______
9. Find the average heartbeat per minute of three mammals.
______
______
10. What does the term biodegradable mean? ______
11. When were the first television pictures transmitted? ______
12. Who developed inoculation as a method of preventing the spread of disease?
______
13. Which world cities lie on fault lines?
______
14. Where and what is the epiglottis?
______

Poster explanations

Objective
Y5. T2. T22.
To plan, compose, edit and refine short non-chronological reports and explanatory texts, using reading as a source, focusing on clarity, conciseness, and impersonal style.

Guided work

1. Before the lesson, enlarge photocopiable page 73 to A3 (one per child). Make copies of photocopiable extract pages 116, 117 and 118 (or reuse those made for the lesson 'Scientific explanations' on page 68). Collect some examples of well-designed posters and prepare an example of a poor poster based on the information on photocopiable page 73 (see 'Plenary', below).

2. Re-read with the class the three explanatory texts (pages 116, 117, 118). Remind the children that an explanatory text is a non-fiction resource offering the reader an explanation as to how something functions. Highlight the key features (impersonal style, technical vocabulary, generalised statements, passive voice and the use of hypothetical questions).

3. Tell the children that they will be working on an explanation of a cyclic process. Ask the children what cyclic processes they have studied in science (the human life cycle, the life cycle of a plant, the water cycle).

4. Take the example of the life cycle of a plant, modelling this on the board as a cyclic process. Illustrate germination, growth, flowers, pollination, fertilisation and seed dispersal. Around the illustrations, add explanatory text using: impersonal style; generalised statements (for example, Warmth and moisture encourage the germination of seeds); technical vocabulary (pollination, dispersal); passive voice (Seeds are dispersed); hypothetical language (Why do plants produce fruit?). Use clear and concise text.

Independent work

- Make sure each child has a partner to work with and an enlarged copy of photocopiable page 73. Ask the children to identify the process illustrated (the water cycle) and to explain it to their talking partners.
- Tell the children that they are to create a poster that explains the water cycle, designed for their peer group. Look together at your selection of 'good' posters and identify their features, such as an eye-catching design or sub-headings. Tell the children that their poster must fit the criteria of an explanatory text: impersonal style, passive voice, technical vocabulary and generalised statements. Allow the children access to scientific books or websites for their research.
- Encourage the children to plan and revise their additions to the poster before they commit to the final version. Praise children who include technical vocabulary, concise explanations of the process and examples of the passive voice.

Plenary

- Show the children the poster you prepared earlier, which does not use technical vocabulary, the passive voice or concise explanations. As a group, read, evaluate and assess this poor example. Ask: How could the author of this poster make improvements?

Further challenge
- Ask the children to design, edit, refine and make posters for a variety of other processes. These might answer questions such as: Why do we experience an eclipse? Why do we experience earthquakes? Why do some objects float?

Poster explanations

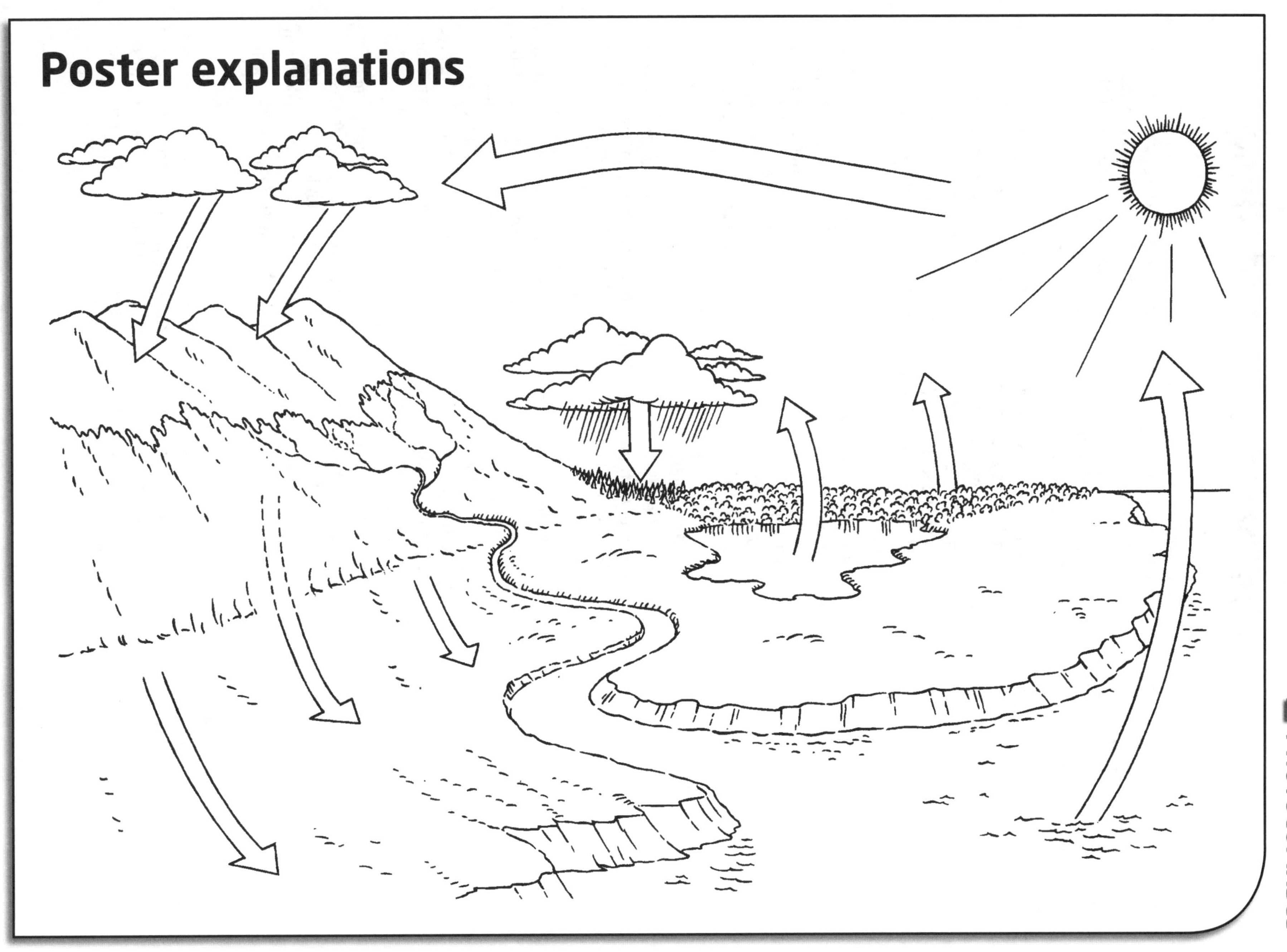

Historical point of view

Objective
Y5. T3. T3.
To change point of view, eg tell incident or describe a situation from the point of view of another character or perspective.

Guided work

1. Prepare the drama prompt cards on photocopiable page 75 prior to the lesson, adding any other historical events that the children have studied recently and removing those that the children have not studied. Enlarge and then laminate the cards individually, so that one prompt can be given to each group. Enlarge the photocopiable extract on page 112.

2. Begin the lesson by explaining to the children that they will be describing a famous event from the point of view of several characters, who will each talk about the event from his or her own perspective. Explain to the children that stories are often told from the perspective of one or two major characters. Tell the children that their dramas will allow the other, often subsidiary, characters to narrate the story from their perspective.

3. Use the extract from Roald Dahl's classic *The BFG* on page 112. Read together the enlarged text. Discuss with the children the main character, Sophie, and agree that the whole story is narrated from her perspective. Ask the children to suggest how the story would be different if it were told from the perspective of the BFG himself, or another character from the book. Give the children time to discuss these options with a partner.

Independent work

- Explain to the children that they will be working in small groups to act out famous stories from history. Reassure the children that these are stories that they have studied, so they will already know the plot and the endings.

- Tell the children to assign a character from the story to every person in their group. They must improvise a short sketch, which is based upon the prompt. Hand out your prepared drama prompts, one for each group. Encourage the children to be innovative in their choice of characters and ensure that they give each character in their drama a distinct personality. Point out to the children that they have the opportunity to give a pivotal role to a character who is usually unimportant.

- As the children improvise and develop their dramas, circulate among the groups and question the children while they remain in character. Ask Henry VIII's advisers why they are supporting him. Challenge Caesar's generals about invading another foreign land. Praise the children who can remain in character and tell the story from their own perspective.

Plenary

- End the lesson by asking several of the children to retell the story they dramatised – from the perspective of their character. Praise those children who develop the role of their own character within the drama and those who express the emotions of their character, as well as showing empathy towards the 'main' character.

Further challenge
- Use circle time to identify events of importance to the children and, through discussion, encourage the children to see these from a variety of perspectives. This would be a sensitive way to deal with the children's reactions both to personal issues and to potentially controversial topics (religion, war or terrorism).

Historical point of view

Henry VIII and his advisers have decided that he should divorce Catherine of Aragon.

Caesar has heard of a land called England – which he wants as part of the Roman empire.

Florence Nightingale has just arrived at the Barrack Hospital in Scutari, a suburb on the Asian side of Constantinople.

The athletes are gathering to compete in the first Olympics.

Nazi troops have invaded France and now threaten the English coast.

The miners have gone on strike. Picket lines are everywhere.

Roman centurions are building a long wall under the instruction of their emperor Hadrian.

Many Irish people are emigrating to America because of a potato famine. The journey across the ocean is long and dangerous.

Robert Wintour, Christophor Wright, Thomas Percy, Guy Fawkes, Francis Tresham and Thomas Bates are plotting to overthrow King James I.

The Pharaoh Khufu has ordered the construction of a great pyramid at Giza in Egypt.

Older literature

Objective
Y5. T3. T6.
To explore the challenge and appeal of older literature through: listening to older literature being read aloud; discussing differences in language used.

Guided work

1. Before the lesson, make copies of photocopiable extract page 119, one per child. Begin the lesson by explaining to the children that they will be listening to an extract from the famous Shakespearean play, Henry V, which gives a fictional account of real events that took place in the 1400s. Ask the children about their previous experience of Shakespeare's writing. Praise children who can name other works or know some famous quotations.

3. Set the scene for the extract. King Henry V of England has made a claim to the crown of France and in this scene a huge fleet of 1500 ships has landed at the French port of Harfleur – this real event took place in August 1415. The King is speaking to his troops as they prepare to attack. Read the text aloud to the children with emotion and intonation. Point out that it is a poem and highlight the poetic features (descriptive language and imagery, regular number of syllables per line).

4. Discuss with the children the subject matter of the play, reminding them that Henry is leading his soldiers into battle. Discuss the purpose of the speech, which is motivational – like a football manager motivating his team to win.

5. Read the speech aloud a second time and discuss each section in turn. Talk about the content of the play, which:

- contrasts a man being humble in times of peace (modest stillness and humility) and like an animal in times of war (imitate the action of the tiger)
- describes the men's physical preparation for their task (set the teeth and stretch the nostril wide)
- appeals for them to be as brave as their fathers (who fought and sheathed their own swords) and to make their families proud (dishonour not your mothers)
- appeals for loyalty to their country (good yeoman, whose limbs were made in England)
- recognises that they are ready and motivated to fight (straining upon the start)
- gives the final instruction to charge (upon this charge cry...).

Independent work

- Distribute copies of photocopiable page 77. Ask the children to investigate the meaning of some of the archaic words and phrases. Encourage the children to keep reading the speech aloud: the meanings of individual words will become more apparent within the context of a whole sentence.

Plenary

- Discuss the phrases listed on photocopiable page 77, and ask the children to give their contemporary equivalents. For homework, give the children a copy of the photocopiable extract on page 119 and ask them to rewrite this famous speech for a present-day audience of their peers.

Further challenge
- Give the children extracts from other Shakespearean plays: Romeo and Juliet, II.2 (But soft!...); Macbeth, II.1 (Is this a dagger...); Julius Caesar III.2 (Friends, Romans, countrymen...). Ask the children to read and perform these in small groups, discussing examples of archaic English and attempting to understand them fully.

Older literature

■ Do you know what these Shakespearean phrases mean? Write what you think would be a modern equivalent for each one.

Shakespearean phrase	Modern equivalent
unto the breach	
stiffen the sinews	
fair nature	
o'erwhelm	
doth	
stretch the nostril wide	
from morn till even	
sheathed	
dishonour not	
attest	
beget you	
men of grosser blood	
yeomen	
mettle	
which I doubt not	
base	
hath not	
noble lustre	
straining upon the start	
the game's afoot	

Letters

Objective
Y5. T3. T12.
To read and evaluate letters, eg from newspapers, magazines, intended to inform, protest, complain, persuade, considering (i) how they are set out (ii) how language is used, eg to gain attention, respect, manipulate.

Guided work
1. Before the lesson, ensure you have one copy of photocopiable page 79 per child. Begin the lesson by asking the children if they have ever written letters. Ask: Who did you write to? What was the purpose of the letter? What format did you use? Did you receive a response?

2. Build up a list of different purposes for letter writing, for example: complaints, requests, invitations, thanks, maintaining friendship. Discuss with the children which of these types of letter would most likely provide examples of formal letter writing.

3. Provide the children with copies of photocopiable page 79 and ask them to skim read both letters of complaint. Encourage basic annotation of key facts. Ask the children to summarise the facts. (Luke bought a game that does not work and the shop would not refund or exchange his game.)

4. Examine the first letter and ask the children to comment critically on it. Discuss with the children the informal nature of the letter, the overuse of the pronoun 'I', the colloquialism 'OK', the basic sentence structure and vocabulary. Ask the children how professional the letter sounds and elicit comments on how seriously the letter will be taken.

5. Next, read and comment on the second letter, which makes the same complaint. Highlight the opening sentence, which provides the background detail. Ask the children how it is that this letter sounds more formal and professional? What examples of vocabulary represent an improvement on the first letter? ('Purchase' rather than 'buy', 'assistance' rather than 'sort it out' and so on.) Ask the children which letter is more likely to receive a prompt and meaningful response.

Independent work
- Ask the children to concentrate on the second letter of complaint. Invite them to highlight general words and phrases that they could use when writing their own letter of complaint.
- Instruct the children to summarise each paragraph, and then to turn these annotations into a general writing frame that could be used for any letter of complaint. For example: Paragraph one explains the background behind the event or situation; Paragraph two is the complaint itself; Paragraph three is an explanation as to what you have done about it; Paragraph four/five says what response you would like.

Plenary
- Review the children's writing frames for letters of complaint and try these out for all letters of complaint. Suggest a variety of causes for complaint (an important letter lost in the post; a train breaking down and causing a serious delay; damaged goods from a shop; poor customer service). Working orally, apply the writing frames to each one.

Further challenge
- Ask the children to plan and write their own letters of complaint (about, for example, bad service in a restaurant, a delayed bus or train causing a missed appointment, late delivery of an important parcel, or a missing letter), using their own writing frames. They may use general words and phrases from photocopiable page 79, as necessary.

Letters

to the manager
I bought a game from your shop on Saturday when I was shopping with my Mum.
I had saved up my pocket money and I wanted the game for ages. When I got the
game home I tried to play it on my computer but it wouldn't load. I was unhappy
and my mum said that I could bring it back to the shop for you to sort it out.
I came back to the shop and a different man was on the till. He told me that the
game was ok and it must be the way I was loading it. I felt bad because my mum
wasn't with me and I didn't know what so say.
When I got home my Mum said that I should write down my complaint, so I am.
Please write back to me.
From
Luke Jones aged 11

Luke Jones
21 North Drive
Applewood Fields
Tollington TL21 3RR

Monday 15th November

Dear Customer Services,

On Saturday 13th November I visited your store on the High Street in Appleton to purchase the latest edition of the game *Football Manager* for my computer. Having saved my pocket money for several weeks, I was pleased that I could finally afford it.

On returning home, I began experiencing difficulty when I attempted to load the game. The message "*insufficient data*" appeared on my screen. I took the game from the machine and attempted to load it again, taking great care to follow the instruction manual. The game refused to load and the error message appeared again.

On the advice of my mother, I revisited your shop the following day to ask for advice and assistance with this problem. The assistant operating the till initially overlooked me as I waited in the queue, choosing to serve adults before he turned his attention to me. When he finally decided to serve me he was unsympathetic to my problem, suggesting that I had not followed the instruction manual properly. My request for an exchange or a refund was refused and I left the shop.

I strongly feel that I was treated unfairly by your assistant due to the fact that I am a minor. My complaint was not taken seriously and remains unresolved.

I trust you will investigate this matter thoroughly. I look forward to receiving your prompt reply.

Yours faithfully
Mr L. Jones

From story to stage

Objective
Y6. T1. T9.
To prepare a short section of a story as a script, eg using stage directions, location/setting.

Guided work

1. Before the lesson, make copies of photocopiable extract page 120 and photocopiable page 81 (one of each per child).

2. Begin the lesson by explaining to the children that they will be reading an extract from a famous novel by the author Lewis Carroll. Have the children previously heard of Lewis Carroll? Can they name any of his poems? ('Jabberwocky', 'The Walrus and the Carpenter', 'How Doth the Little Crocodile?', 'Beautiful Soup', 'You Are Old, Father William'.)

3. Explain to the children that they will be working on an extract from *Alice in Wonderland* about the Mad Hatter's tea party; the children may be familiar with this piece from the book, film, cartoon or television. Their task for the lesson will be to turn this famous extract into a playscript. Discuss the children's previous experiences of reading playscripts. Ask: What features are common to all playscripts? List on the board the key features (scene setting, the formatting of speech using the colon, brackets for stage directions, the use of the present tense for narrative sections and so on).

4. Distribute and read with the children the photocopiable extract on page 120. Briefly discuss the text. Ask the children: Are you familiar with the story? Who are the characters? What actually happens in the extract? What would the characters' first impressions be of one another? What might happen next?

Independent work

- Provide the children with copies of photocopiable page 81. Explain to the children that this is the beginning of a playscript that is to be written, based on the extract they have just read.

- Compare the beginning of the playscript to the beginning of the text extract. The playscript begins with scene setting: Curtain opens upon a large table, set out under a tree... The details are the same, but the tense has changed from past to present and there is an awareness that this scene takes place in front of an audience.

- Ask the children to continue the playscript, based closely on the extract. Provide lined paper for them to use as continuation sheets, if necessary. As the children work, encourage them to use Carroll's adverbs when directing the actors. Remind them to qualify the characters' speech using adverbs.

Plenary

- Put the children into groups of four and allow them to read through their playscripts, taking one character each. As they read each playscript, the children should switch roles so that by the end of the lesson each child has played every role. Encourage the children to discuss similarities and differences in one another's playscripts.

Further challenge
- Allow the children to read more of the novel and make a detailed comparison between one chapter of the novel and a television or cartoon version of the story.

From story to stage

Alice in Wonderland: Act II Scene 1

(Curtain opens upon a large table, set out under a tree in front of the house, and the March Hare and the Hatter are seated at it. A Dormouse is sitting between them, fast asleep, and the other two are resting their elbows on it. The three characters are all crowded together at one corner of the table.)

Alice (entering stage left, looks at the scene, frowns disapprovingly; she addresses the audience): Very uncomfortable for the Dormouse, only, as it's asleep, I suppose it doesn't mind.
Hatter (realising Alice is approaching): No room! No room!
March Hare: No! There's no room here!
Alice (indignantly): There's plenty of room!

March Hare (encouragingly): ____________________

Continue on lined paper if necessary.

Biography of a scientist

Objective
Y6. T1. T14.
To develop the skills of biographical writing in role, adopting distinctive voices, eg of historical characters.

Guided work

1. Before the lesson, ensure you have one copy of photocopiable page 83 per child.

2. Begin the lesson by explaining to the children that they will be writing the biography of a famous physicist. Ask the children what they know about Albert Einstein and his work. Explain that he was a famous scientist who discovered the theory of relativity (summarised by the equation $e=mc^2$). This theory tells us that the mathematical relationship between energy, mass and the speed of light is always the same.

3. Ask the children to recall any previous biographies or autobiographies they have written. Discuss the features of a biographical text. (Personal details, chronological order and so on.) Compare and contrast biography and autobiography. Ensure the children understand that an autobiography is written by the person himself (Albert Einstein, for example). An autobiography is more likely to include opinions and feelings in addition to descriptions of the key events.

4. Distribute and read through photocopiable page 83. Discuss the format: short contracted sentences, based on key facts and dates. Model for the children how this information could be transferred to a biographical text. For example:

> Albert Einstein was born in 1879 in Ulm, Germany, the son of Hermann Einstein and his wife Pauline. The Einstein family moved to Pavia, Italy, in 1894 - leaving the 15-year-old Albert in Munich to finish school. However, he lasted only a month before joining his family in Italy. At the age of 16, Albert sat a university entrance exam. Although he was an able mathematician and scientist, he found the arts section of the exam challenging and on this first occasion he failed. Despite this disappointment, Albert remained determined to continue his education and in the same year, 1895, he set off for the Swiss town of Aarau to finish high school.

Independent work

- Ask the children to continue the biography, encouraging them to re-order the sentences and to use more descriptive vocabulary. Tell the children to find inventive ways of indicating the passage of time (ten years later, when he was 30... and so on).

- Encourage the children to edit their work as they write - looking for general writing features, such as: connecting words and phrases, variety of sentence structure and the use of good vocabulary.

Plenary

- Ask the children to close their books and retell as much biographical information about Albert Einstein as they can recall. Briefly review how this information would be different if it were autobiographical. (It would use personal pronouns and there would be more detail on thoughts, feelings and emotions.)

Further challenge
- Ask the children to interview one another and then write brief biographies. Allow them to focus equally on the speaking and listening elements of the formal interview process and on the written elements of the final biography.

Biography of a scientist

The life of Albert Einstein: a time line

1879: Albert Einstein is born to Hermann and Pauline Einstein in Ulm, a town near Munich, Germany.

1894: The Einsteins to Pavia, Italy. Albert stays to finish school in Munich. He only lasts a month without his family and then joins them in Italy.

1895: Albert sits a university entrance exam but fails on the arts section. His family send him to the Swiss town of Aarau to finish high school.

1896: Albert graduates high school and enrols in a polytechnic in Zurich.

1898: Albert meets fellow student Mileva Maric and falls in love.

1900: Albert graduates from the polytechnic.

1901: Albert becomes a Swiss citizen.

1902: Hermann Einstein becomes ill and dies.

1903: Albert and Mileva marry.

1904: Albert and Mileva have a son called Hans Albert.

1905: Albert Einstein publishes an article entitled 'On the electrodynamics of moving bodies' in a leading German physics journal. He applies his theory to mass and energy and formulates the famous equation $e=mc^2$.

1910: The Einsteins have a second son, Eduard.

1911: Albert and his family move to Prague where Albert is given a professorship at the university there.

1912: The family then moves to Zurich where Albert is again made a professor.

1914: Einstein become director of the Kaiser Wilhelm institute in Berlin. He and Mileva begin divorce proceedings.

1915: The general theory of relativity is finished.

1919: Albert remarries – his second wife is called Elsa. A solar eclipse proves that Einstein's theory of relativity works.

1921: Albert Einstein is awarded the Nobel Prize for physics.

1933: At the height of his fame, and as a Jew in Nazi Germany, Einstein decides to sail to America with his wife Elsa. They settle in New Jersey.

1936: Elsa dies.

1939: The Second World War begins. Einstein writes to the US president urging nuclear research, as Germany may be developing the atomic bomb.

1955: Einstein dies of heart failure.

Nonsense poetry

Objectives
Y6. T2. T4.
To investigate humorous verse: how poets play with meanings; nonsense words and how meaning can be made of them; where the appeal lies.

Y6. T2. T9.
To increase familiarity with significant poets and writers of the past.

Guided work

1. Begin the lesson by asking the children for their views on poetry. Ask: What poetry do you enjoy? Do you have a favourite poet? What other poets can you think of? Can you name any of the poems that these poets have written? Do you prefer rhyming or non-rhyming poems?

2. Tell the children that today they will be reading humorous poetry. Ask the children if they know of any poets who specialise in this genre (Edward Lear, Lewis Carroll, Spike Milligan).

3. Provide each child with a copy of the three nonsense poems on photocopiable page 121. Have an enlarged copy as a teacher resource and read the poems together. Identify why each of the poems would be seen as nonsense (nonsense words in 'On the Ning Nang Nong'; unlikely comparison of a bat to a tea tray in 'Twinkle Twinkle'; impossible event in Edward Lear's poem). Discuss the meaning behind each poem: can the children unpick what is being described? (For example, in the Lear poems, a lady's nose grows so long that she cannot see the end of it!)

4. Ask the children to speculate as to why these poems may be considered humorous. Why do they appeal to the reader? (They enable us to use our imagination when visualising the nonsensical images described.)

Independent work

- Hand out copies of photocopiable page 85. Tell the children to look closely at the images drawn by Edward Lear. Ask the children to work in table groups to mind-map on large sheets of paper all the words and phrases that they can think of, relating to the pictures. Encourage the children to add verbs as well as adjectives and nouns.

- Give the children five minutes to mind-map the images and then ask them to take one or two examples and turn them into nonsense words. For example, they may merge two words together to come up with a nonsense word (thus brilliant and colourful become brillourful or parrot and cat become paracat).

- Ask the children to write a short stanza inspired by the story told in the illustrations. Those children who require support may follow the format of another poem – a limerick, for example.

Plenary

- Allow the children to share their poetry. Have any of them successfully written some humorous verse? Did they make each other laugh or smile? Discuss the appeal of their poetry.

Further challenge
- Ask the children to read and comment on more poems by Edward Lear, Lewis Carroll and Spike Milligan and then, working in small friendship groups, to produce a polished performance of a favourite. They might choose to sing parts of the poem, add percussion instruments or assign different lines to different readers.

Nonsense poetry

Challenging poetry

Objectives
Y6. T2. T6.
To read and interpret poems in which meanings are implied or multi-layered; to discuss, interpret challenging poems with others.

Y6. T2. T9.
To increase familiarity with significant poets and writers of the past.

Guided work

1. Explain to the children that they will be studying two well-known (and quite difficult) war poems: the children will need to read them carefully and think hard about their meaning.

2. Discuss reading techniques used previously when examining poetry. Remind the children to consider the theme of the poem. If there are several verses, the children should examine each in turn – looking for changes in theme, style or format. Where possible, the children should annotate the poetry as they read.

3. Provide the children with copies of 'Dulce et Decorum Est' by Wilfred Owen on photocopiable extract page 122. Give the children some information about the poet, who was a soldier in the First World War. He volunteered for the forces in 1915 and was soon at the front line, where he was shocked at the conditions. He started writing poetry in 1917, when he was injured and spent time in hospital. He returned to the trenches in 1918 and won the Military Cross. Shortly afterwards he was shot and killed.

4. Read the poem aloud, as the children follow each line. Read it again, this time encouraging the children to join in. Ask: What is the theme of the poem? (That there is no glory in war.) What evidence is there to support this? (The men are too exhausted to withstand the danger around them: Men marched asleep, Gas! clumsy helmets.)

5. Read and discuss each section, using the annotations on photocopiable page 87 to guide the discussion. Encourage the children to look for themes, meaning and key vocabulary as they continue to annotate their own copies. Engage all the children in the discussion by asking open questions and allow paired discussion among the children before asking for a response.

Independent work

- Distribute copies of 'The Soldier' by Rupert Brooke on photocopiable extract page 123. Tell the children that Rupert Brooke joined the navy at the beginning of the First World War and witnessed the siege of Antwerp before writing a set of five famous sonnets called '1914' – of which this is one. He had seen the devastation caused by war but kept it at a distance and denied its realities. He died in 1915 on his way to fight in Turkey.

- Explain to the children that they must now annotate this second poem as they did the first. Encourage them to discuss in pairs the themes of each section and the style of the poet. Use photocopiable page 87 to support children who are struggling.

Plenary

- Discuss similarities and differences between the two poems. Both are war poems but they have different themes: Owen questions the glorification of war; Brooke suggests that dying in 'a foreign field' leaves there a piece of England's goodness.

Further challenge
- Encourage the children to explore other war poetry, possibly from different conflicts such as the conflict in the Balkans. Poetry of this nature could be used for Remembrance Day services in school.

Challenging poetry

Dulce et Decorum Est – Wilfred Owen

Bent double, like old beggars under sacks,
Knock-kneed, coughing like hags, we cursed through sludge,
Till on the haunting flares we turned our backs
And towards our distant rest began to trudge.
Men marched asleep. Many had lost their boots
But limped on, blood-shod. All went lame; all blind;
Drunk with fatigue; deaf even to the hoots
Of tired, outstripped Five-Nines that dropped behind.

Gas! Gas! Quick, boys! – An ecstasy of fumbling,
Fitting the clumsy helmets just in time;
But someone still was yelling out and stumbling,
And flound'ring like a man on fire or lime...
Dim, through the misty panes and thick green light,
As under a green sea, I saw him drowning.
In all my dreams, before my helpless sight,
He plunges at me, guttering, choking, drowning.

If in some smothering dreams you too could pace
Behind the wagon that we flung him in,
And watch the white eyes writhing in his face,
His hanging face, like a devil's sick of sin;
If you could hear, at every jolt, the blood
Come gargling from the froth-corrupted lungs,
Obscene as cancer, bitter as the cud
Of vile, incurable sores on innocent tongues,
My friend, you would not tell with such high zest
To children ardent for some desperate glory,
The old Lie: Dulce et decorum est
Pro patria mori.

Annotations:

- Describes the movement of troops away from the front line, during WW1 (1914–18). These were young men yet they are referred to as being like old men or women (hags). → Bent double, like old beggars under sacks,
- By 'distant rest' did the poet mean permanent rest (ie death)? → And towards our distant rest began to trudge.
- 'Blood-shod' is dehumanising. 'Shod' is more commonly used to refer to horses. → But limped on, blood-shod.
- 'Ecstasy' was a medical term referring to a nervous state in which a person's mind is obsessed with one idea. → Gas! Gas! Quick, boys! – An ecstasy of fumbling,
- The poet can see the gas consuming them. He sees one man unable to put on his gas mask in time. → He plunges at me, guttering, choking, drowning.
- The reader is asked to imagine following the dying man once he is on the cart. → Behind the wagon that we flung him in,
- Description of the physical symptoms the man is experiencing. → Obscene as cancer, bitter as the cud
- The men are really tired – so tired they don't hear artillery shells (calibre 5.9") being dropped behind them. → Of tired, outstripped Five-Nines that dropped behind.
- They are so tired that they struggle to put on their gas masks. → Fitting the clumsy helmets just in time;
- Metaphor of drowning used to describe a man in a state of exhaustion. → Dim, through the misty panes and thick green light,
- A haunting image which the poet will remember. → In all my dreams, before my helpless sight,
- The repeating taste of vile sores on the tongue. → Of vile, incurable sores on innocent tongues,
- These lines question whether children who are desperate for the glory of war should be encouraged in such sentiments. → My friend, you would not tell with such high zest
- Latin translated means, 'It is lovely and noble to die on behalf of your country.' → The old Lie: Dulce et decorum est

The Soldier – Rupert Brook

If I should die, think only this of me:
That there's some corner of a foreign field
That is forever England.
There shall be
In that rich earth a richer dust concealed;
A dust whom England bore, shaped, made aware,
Gave, once, her flowers to love, her ways to roam,
A body of England's, breathing English air,
Washed by the rivers, blest by suns of home.

And think, this heart, all evil shed away,
A pulse in the eternal mind, no less
Gives somewhere back the thoughts by England given;
Her sights and sounds; dreams happy as her day;
And laughter, learnt of friends; and gentleness,
In hearts at peace, under an English heaven.

Annotations:

- Example of conditional. → If I should die, think only this of me:
- Examples of personification. → In that rich earth a richer dust concealed;
- Reinforcement of patriotism by repetition of 'England', 'England's' and 'English'. → A dust whom England bore, shaped, made aware,
- England given female identity; personification. → Gave, once, her flowers to love, her ways to roam,
- The poet's heart is no longer engaged in war but in remembering happy thoughts of home. He is at peace. → Gives somewhere back the thoughts by England given;
- If the poet dies, the place where he is buried will then have his body – which is a piece of England. → That is forever England.
- The earth there will be richer due to the presence of his English remains. → In that rich earth a richer dust concealed;
- A very rural environment is described. → A body of England's, breathing English air,
- Wherever the poet is, he is passing on elements of England. → Gives somewhere back the thoughts by England given;

Writing arguments

Objectives

Y6. T2. T18.
To construct effective arguments: developing a point of view logically and effectively; supporting and illustrating points persuasively; anticipating possible objections; harnessing the known views, interests and feelings of the audience.

Y6. T2. T19.
To write a balanced report of a controversial issue: summarising fairly the competing views; analysing the strengths and weaknesses of different positions.

Guided work

1. Before the lesson, make copies of photocopiable extract page 43 and photocopiable page 89 (one of each per child).

2. Begin by explaining to the children that they will be writing a speech designed to persuade the audience to agree with them. Ask the children to think of situations in which they may wish to persuade others. Explore a variety of contexts – ranging from the informal (asking parents for more pocket money or permission to stay up late), to the formal (election speeches, a barrister summing up in court, a headteacher addressing an assembly).

3. Distribute copies of photocopiable page 43 and re-read it with the children. Highlight the persuasive way in which the different points are made. Examine the ways in which opposing arguments are tackled and known views are addressed.

Independent work

- Explain to the children that they are to write a speech on a topic that they are passionate about. Offer some controversial questions that will evoke strong opinions and ask the children to suggest more. (Should pupils be allowed mobile phones in school? Are zoos cruel to animals? Should children be forced to wear school uniform? Should school dinners offer a set healthy menu? Should the minimum driving age be increased to 21? Should copying music be a criminal offence? Should parents be punished when children play truant?)

- Ask the children: What language features should your argument include? (Connectives, present tense, emotive language, technically accurate information.) Write on the board the children's suggestions.

- Let the children begin writing their speeches, using four paragraphs comprising:

  - an introduction (introduce yourself and state the purpose of the argument)
  - an outline of your side of the argument (take one point at a time; explain each point fully; illustrate it with examples)
  - an anticipation of possible objections (take one point at a time and explain objections; include resolutions for each objection, if possible)
  - a conclusion (restate your strongest argument; finish with a memorable ending).

- Allow the children to record their speeches on audio or videotape. When the children listen to their own recordings, encourage self-assessment – particularly of the language used.

Plenary

- Distribute copies of photocopiable page 89. Ask the children to evaluate this speech, which is meant to deliver a balanced argument about whether smoking should be banned in public places. Does it succeed? If not, why not? How could the speech be improved? Invite the children to write on the sheet their suggested improvements, then to share these, paragraph by paragraph, with the class.

Further challenge

- Change the focus from speech to letter, asking the children to write a letter about their controversial issue to a magazine or newspaper. Discuss the need for a different format and consider how the introductory and concluding paragraphs will need to be changed to fit the new audience and medium.

Writing arguments

A poor example of a written argument

■ Make amendments to this text to improve the quality of the argument by refining the language and by adding any other points that you consider to be convincing.

Hello, my name is Adrian and I was asked to tell you why I think people shouldn't smoke in public places like parks and on the street as well as in pubs and restaurants.

I think smoking is bad for you and some smokers make other people smoke by passive smoking. If the people in charge banned smoking in public we would all be healthy. Also it is expensive.

Some people will think that it is not fair and that they should be allowed to do what they want without being told what to do. Lots of people have smoked for a long time and wouldn't be able to give up so there would be nowhere that they could go and smoke except in their own house.

I don't think people should be allowed to smoke in public because it smells bad and it is not fair on the rest of us that don't smoke.

Cyclic poetry

Objectives

Y6. T3. T2.
To discuss how linked poems relate to one another by themes, format and repetition, eg cycle of poems about the seasons.

Y6. T3. T3.
To describe and evaluate the style of an individual poet.

Guided work

1. Before the lesson, make copies of photocopiable extract pages 124 and 125 (one of each per child); also make enlarged copies or OHTs of both pages. Find another poem by one of these four poets (Eric Finney, Jo Peters, Benjamin Zephaniah or Roger McGough), and make copies for use in the Plenary.

2. Distribute the copies of photocopiable extract pages 124 and 125 and ask the children to skim read all four poems. Discuss the common theme: seasons. Ask: Which is your favourite poem and why? Which do you like the least? Encourage the children to justify their opinions with evidence from the text. (I like 'Reasons for Seasons' because of the positive seasonal imagery: butterflies in spring; jelly in summer; squirrels in autumn; snow in winter. I love the personification of the seasons in 'The Fight of the Year' – 'Winter comes out of his corner looking groggy'.)

3. Display your enlarged copies and read the poems together, one at a time. Ask the children to help you to annotate each. For example:

- 'Simple Seasons' (Eric Finney) is an acrostic with one word per line and a maximum of two sentences per verse; it describes each season simply.
- 'Seasons' (Jo Peters) is another acrostic: each verse describes one season and its effects on nature; lines 2, 4 and 6 rhyme throughout.
- 'Reasons for Seasons' (Benjamin Zephaniah) centres on the girl, Jialu; each verse describes how she plays in a particular season.
- 'The Fight of the Year' (Roger McGough) uses personification to describe a fight between winter and spring.

4. Ensure that the children understand the seasonal vocabulary; allow them to use dictionaries to check unfamiliar words.

Independent work

- Distribute copies of photocopiable page 91. Ask the children to evaluate all four poems, commenting on the themes, format, repetition, rhyme and style. The children should first re-read the poems separately – then compare them.

- Give the children examples of possible comments, for example: Three of the poems take the seasons one at a time and describe them; the fourth describes the transition from one season to another.

- Invite the children to make personal comments about each poem, supported by evidence from the text. (For example: I really enjoyed 'The Fight of the Year' because Spring defeats Winter using daffodils, primroses, crocuses'.) Encourage them to discuss preferences as they work.

Plenary

- Give the children another poem by one of these four poets. Ask: What message is conveyed? Can you comment on the format or rhythm of the poem? How is it similar/different to this poet's other poem, discussed earlier? The children may use photocopiable page 91 to make notes before sharing their views with the class.

Further challenge

- Set the children the task of finding other seasonal poems by searching anthologies, libraries or the internet (for example: 'Winter Morning' by Ogden Nash; 'The Calendar' by Barbara Euphan Todd; 'December' by Robert Southey). Encourage discussion of these poems and ask the children to evaluate them using the criteria listed on photocopiable page 91.

Cyclic poetry

Title of poem	Poet	Themes of verses	Format	Repetition	Rhyme	Style	Personal comment
Reasons for Seasons	Benjamin Zephaniah						
Simple Seasons	Eric Finney						
Seasons	Jo Peters						
The Fight of the Year	Roger McGough						

Season poems

Objective
Y6. T3. T13.
To write a sequence of poems linked by theme or form.

Guided work

1. This lesson works best as a continuation of the lesson 'Cyclic poetry' on page 90.

2. Begin the lesson by reminding the children of the four seasonal poems on photocopiable extract pages 124 and 125 read and discussed recently. Explain to the children that they will be writing their own seasonal poetry using the acrostic frame used by Eric Finney ('Simple Seasons') and Jo Peters ('Seasons').

3. Split the class into four groups and assign a season to each group. Provide each group with a large piece of paper and ask the children to mind-map their season. Encourage them to think about nature (what is growing, what the weather is like), the senses (smells, sights, sensations, sounds or tastes), seasonal events (Hallowe'en, bonfire night, Divali, Hanukkah, Christmas, new year, Easter, Pesach, Ramadan), their own lives (holidays, school events, recreation) and so on. For example, the children might think about the sense of excitement early on Christmas morning. Ask the children to add as many adjectives and adverbs as they can to these ideas. Give the children ten minutes to mind-map as many concepts as they can think of relating to their season.

4. At the end of the ten minutes, ask the children to report back to the whole group on some of their seasonal features. Check to see that each group has added adjectives to its mind-map. Display the seasonal mind-maps in prominent places around the classroom.

Independent work

- Explain to the children that they are to use these mind-maps as inspiration when writing their own seasonal acrostic poems. Provide each child with a copy of photocopiable page 93 for their poem.

- Begin with spring, asking the children which concepts from the mind-map they would like to include in the first verse of their poem. Discuss the different events, weather and features of nature that evoke images of spring.

- Tell the children that they should choose for themselves the repetition and rhyme scheme of their poem. For example, they may wish to: begin every verse with a similar line (as Benjamin Zephaniah does in 'Reasons for Seasons'); use rhyming couplets, or rhyme every other line; use alliteration, personification, metaphor, simile and so on.

- Allow the children to draft their work first, so that they can reject ideas that do not work. Encourage the children to keep reading their poems aloud so that they can hear how they are developing.

Plenary

- Ask the children to read to the class their favourite verse of their own poem. As the other children listen, ask them to pick out features they enjoy from their classmate's poetry.

Further challenge

- Encourage the children to revise and redraft their poems. Use Microsoft Publisher or another desktop publishing program to collate all the children's poetry into a class anthology, which can be published and distributed around your school.

Season poems

Use the frame below to create your own poem on the seasons.

S ______________________________

P ______________________________

R ______________________________

I ______________________________

N ______________________________

G ______________________________

S ______________________________

U ______________________________

M ______________________________

M ______________________________

E ______________________________

R ______________________________

A ______________________________

U ______________________________

T ______________________________

U ______________________________

M ______________________________

N ______________________________

W ______________________________

I ______________________________

N ______________________________

T ______________________________

E ______________________________

R ______________________________

Writing an extended story

Objective

Y6. T3. T14.
To write an extended story, worked on over time on a theme identified in reading.

Guided work

1. Before the lesson, ensure you have one copy of photocopiable page 95 per child. Make a blank version of the writing frame used below, and photocopy it for the children's use.

2. Begin the lesson by reminding the children of an extended story read recently. This may link to transition work for Key Stage 3, looking at author studies of Michael Morpurgo or Anne Fine. Identify the story genre, discuss how it develops and analyse it using a frame, like this:

	Book title: Kensuke's Kingdom Author: Michael Morpurgo
Introduction	The family decides to leave the conventional lifestyle and sail around the world on a boat called *Peggy Sue.*
Build-up	During a storm, Michael and Stella fall overboard and are stranded on a deserted island.
Main event	Michael is cared for by a strange man called Kensuke, who has lived on the island for years. They become close and Kensuke shares his secrets.
End/resolution	Michael is rescued and reunited with his family, but keeps Kensuke's secrets for years... until now.

3. Ask the children comprehension-style questions relating to your chosen book. For example: How is (a character) introduced? How is (a particular setting) described? What do we learn about (a character) in (a particular passage) or on (a certain page)?

4. Tell the children to plan their own stories in the same genre as the story just discussed. They should use a writing frame similar to the one above, focusing separately on the introduction, build-up, main event and resolution. Distribute copies of photocopiable page 95. Draw the children's attention to the essential features of narrative writing. Make sure they understand that this is a longer writing project. Allow them one whole session to plan their stories.

Independent work

- After the planning is complete, spend one session on each section of the story, providing guidelines for how the writing should be tackled. For example, in the introduction the children need to grab the reader's attention with a good opening (action, description or dialogue) and describe characters in innovative ways.

- Remind the children to read and evaluate their work against the checklist at regular intervals; encourage paired editing. Look for examples of good narrative to share with the class: regularly read aloud short sections, explaining what you like about them (for example, use of metaphor).

Plenary

- End each session by handing out editing pens and asking the children, in pairs, to edit one another's work. Encourage improvement at word and sentence level: for example, adding adverbs to enhance description or changing sentences from active to passive to vary sentence structure.

Further challenge

- Ask the children to read and evaluate each other's completed stories. Compare them with the story that provided the original inspiration and ask the children to compare themselves as writers to the initial author.

Writing an extended story

A checklist for writing good stories

When planning

- Before you start – know the end!
- Keep the plot simple and stick to one genre.
- Don't use friends as characters – develop characters of your own.

When writing

- Grab the reader from the start – use a question, speech or a short sharp sentence at the beginning of the story.
- Introduce the setting and characters at the start through adjectives, for example: *eerie, isolated.*
- Make the reader believe in each character – include emotion and feeling. As you describe events, ask yourself: How is my character feeling?
- Don't tell your readers how to feel: make them feel it themselves through your description. For example: beads of sweat gathered on his forehead, he swallowed hard, took a deep breath and slowly turned the door handle.
- Make the readers want to read on – ask questions, lull them into a false sense of security and then surprise them.
- Connectives will help you to structure your writing – use them for changes in time and so on.
- Vary your sentence structure: use both active and passive verbs, and short and long sentences, reported and direct speech.
- Punctuate accurately: – ! ? ( ) "..." ; , .
- Develop the character; include emotions, thoughts, beliefs, actions.
- Be consistent: don't waver between first and third person, or between past and present tense.
- Pronouns can be confusing if you don't use them carefully. Check that it is clear who 'he' or 'she' is.
- Use a dictionary and a thesaurus to help you find exciting vocabulary that will add to the appeal of your writing.

Reading test: Fiction

Objectives

Y5. T1. T9.
To develop an active attitude towards reading: seeking answers, anticipating events, empathising with characters and imagining events that are described.

Y5. T3. T2.
To identify the point of view from which a story is told and how this affects the reader's response.

Y6. T2. T8.
To analyse the success of texts and writers in evoking particular responses in the reader, eg where suspense is well-built.

Guided work

1. Before the lesson, make copies of photocopiable extract page 126 and photocopiable page 97 (one of each per child).

2. Explain to the children that this lesson will help prepare them for the Key Stage 2 Reading Test. Stress that the Reading Test itself could be made up of texts from several different genres, but today the focus will be on narrative.

3. Tell the children that their initial read through of the story should be as quick as possible, giving them a general sense of the plot, characters and structure. They can return to certain parts later, to read them more thoroughly.

4. Advise the children to use text-marking strategies as they read, for example: they may underline characters' names, or insert a star when there is a change in location or time.

Independent work

- Distribute copies of the extract and photocopiable page 97. Explain to the children that they have 20 minutes in which to answer as many questions as possible. Point out that in the real Reading Test they will have more time (one hour, including reading time), but then they will have to read more text and answer more questions.

- Make sure the children know that not all their answers need to be in full sentences. However, they should provide more detailed answers to questions worth two or three marks.

Plenary

- Mark the reading comprehension with the children, as follows:

1.	Midnight	1 mark
2.	Living people, laughing	2 marks
3.	Seventh	1 mark
4.	He was the driver of the hearse.	1 mark
5.	Levis Jeanswear, Adidas Sportswear and cosmetics	All three = 2 marks two = 1 mark
6.	Her sleep was restless and unsettled. Evidence – 'she wrestled with the duvet', 'she thumped the pillow'	1 mark 1 mark
7.	The author indicated an unexplained noise on the driveway. *Or* By describing the sound so vividly, the reader feels involved.	1 mark
8.	The effect is that the reader reads the sentence quickly and this builds up the tension and suspense of the scene. (Do not accept answers that identify the sentence as complex.)	1 mark 1 mark.
9.	'Peeped between the curtains' 'Pulled the duvet up over her head' 'She heard the gravel in the driveway crunch'	2 marks
10.	Simple answers that state a like or dislike of the text Answers that express a preference and state one reason for it Answers that draw on two or more aspects of the text	1 mark 2 marks 3 marks

Further challenge

- Allow the children to read other examples of past narratives that have appeared in the Key Stage 2 SATs reading booklets, for example: 'The One that Got Away' by Jan Mark or 'You Can Do It' by Theresa Breslin.

Reading test: Fiction

Room For One More

1. At what time did the clock strike? ______________________ (1 mark)

2. What was in the back of the hearse? ______________________

______________________ (2 marks)

3. On what floor did the main character end her shopping? ______________________ (1 mark)

4. Why did the lift attendant look familiar to her? ______________________ (1 mark)

5. Which departments in the shop did she visit? ______________________ (2 marks)

____

6. How was the main character sleeping? Use evidence from the text to support your answer.

____

______________________ (2 marks)

7. "She heard the gravel in the driveway crunch." Why does the author tell us that the gravel crunches? ______________________ (1 mark)

8. "She tugged the curtains so they crossed over, and ran back across the room, and jumped into bed, and pulled the duvet up over her head." Why has the author used so many commas in this sentence?

____

______________________ (2 marks)

9. Find and copy two statements where the author attempts to build suspense or a sense of fear.

____

____

______________________ (2 marks)

10. What is your opinion of this as a scary story? Provide evidence from the text to support your opinion.

____

____

______________________ (3 marks)

Reading test: Non-fiction

Objectives

Y6. T1. T13.
To secure understanding of the features of non-chronological reports.

Y6. T3. T17.
To appraise a text quickly and effectively; to retrieve information from it; to find information quickly and evaluate its value.

Guided work

1. Before the lesson, make copies of photocopiable extract page 127 and photocopiable page 99 (one of each per child).

2. Explain to the children that this lesson will help prepare them for the Key Stage 2 Reading Test. Stress that the Reading Test itself could be made up of texts from several different genres, but today the focus will be on non-fiction writing.

3. When reading and annotating a non-fiction text the children will need first to identify the text type. (Report? Explanation?) Point out that non-fiction texts may perform several functions at once. For example, a letter may be written as a persuasive text. Tell the children that when presented with a non-fiction text they should initially scan and skim read it, looking for headings, sub-headings or information in boxes. They should then read it carefully and highlight key facts.

Independent work

- Distribute copies of photocopiable extract page 127. Allow the children five minutes to skim read it and begin highlighting key information. Then distribute photocopiable page 99.

- Explain that they have 15 minutes, within which they should answer as many questions as possible. Point out that in the real Reading Test they will have more time (one hour, including reading time), but then they will have to read more text and answer more questions.

- Make sure the children know that not all their answers need to be in full sentences. However, they should provide more detailed answers to questions worth two or three marks. If there is a question that the children cannot answer, they should move swiftly on to the next one. Recommend to the children that, if they finish the test early, they should use the time to check their answers.

- Provide the children with time prompts. In particular, you should let them know when they have only five minutes remaining.

Plenary

- Mark the work with the children, allowing them instant feedback.

	Answer	Marks
1.	It has a headline; subheadings; a picture, and details events.	2 marks for three, 1 mark for two
2.	David Beckham	1 mark
3.	On Welsh rugby team, 23 years old, plays for Ospreys, boyfriend of Charlotte Church	3 marks for any three
4.	They battled and were beaten. (Do not accept *they were bruised.*)	1 mark
5.	He was not selected.	1 mark
6.	Debut – first (match played).	1 mark
	Season – a period of time (when matches take place)	1 mark
	Tour – the team visits other stadiums and plays matches away from home	1 mark
	Coach – an expert who provides instruction	1 mark
7.	It was the highlight of the season for him.	1 mark

Further challenge

- Ask the children which non-fiction text types they feel least confident with and then provide them with examples of these, to read and discuss. Different examples can be found on The Qualification and Curriculum Authority's Testbase CD-ROM, which is a bank of previous SATs questions.

Reading test: Non-fiction

Welsh Star Ready to Shine

1. How is this web page similar to a newspaper?

____

____ (2 marks)

2. Who is Gavin Henson compared with?

____ (1 mark)

3. Find three facts about Gavin Henson from the article.

____

____

____

____ (3 marks)

4. "Bruising tour of New Zealand" What does the author mean by this?

____ (1 mark)

5. Why was Henson not involved in the first Test in Christchurch?

____ (1 mark)

6. Here are four words from the article; write a definition for each:

Debut ______________________________________ (1 mark)

Season _____________________________________ (1 mark)

Tour _______________________________________ (1 mark)

Coach ______________________________________ (1 mark)

7. "I was delighted to start the second Test, that crowned a great season for me."

What does the speaker mean by this?

____

____

____ (1 mark)

Reading test: Poetry

Objectives

Y6. T2. T3.
To recognise how poets manipulate words: for their quality of sound; for their connotations; for multiple layers of meaning.

Y6. T2. T5.
To analyse how messages are conveyed in poetry.

Y6. T3. T4.
To comment critically on the overall impact of a poem, showing how language and themes have been developed.

Guided work

1. Before the lesson, make copies of photocopiable extract page 128 and photocopiable page 101 (one of each per child).

2. Explain to the children that this lesson will help prepare them for their Reading Test. Stress that the Reading Test itself could be made up of texts from several different genres, but today the focus will be on poetry.

3. Draw the analogy between understanding a poem and solving a puzzle; meanings are not always obvious and need interpretation. Advise the children to read the poem once, then re-read it to confirm initial thoughts. Encourage them to text-mark by drawing boxes around verses, adding notes on themes and/or annotating the text with key words, summarising meaning.

Independent work

- Distribute copies of photocopiable extract page 128 and photocopiable page 101. Explain to the children that they have 15 minutes to answer as many questions as possible. Point out that in the real Reading Test they will have more time (one hour, including reading time), but then they will have to read more text and answer more questions.

- Make sure the children know that not all their answers need to be in full sentences. However, they should provide more detailed answers to questions worth two or three marks.

Plenary

- Review and discuss the questions with the children.

	Answer	Marks
1.	War	1 mark
2.	The soldiers are running/moving/charging towards the enemy.	1 mark
3.	'Into the valley'	1 mark
4.	He is explaining that soldiers must do their duty	1 mark
	and die in the process if necessary.	1 mark
5.	'Was there a man dismayed?'	
	'Some one had blundered'	
	'Valley of Death'	
	'Half a league, half a league, Half a league onward'	any three = 3 marks
6.	'They that had fought so well',	
	'Boldly they rode and well'	
	'O the wild charge they made!'	any two = 2 marks
7.	The 600 are charging a whole army.	1 mark
	they are using sabres (swords) against gunners	1 mark
8.	The other army is Cossack and Russian.	both for 1 mark
9.	'Not the six hundred' (by implication, this means *less than* 600)	1 mark
10.	Expresses possible opinion with no evidence from text	1 mark
	Expresses opinion with one quote explained from text	2 marks
	Expresses poet's opinion with several linked examples	3 marks

(Example of a 3-mark answer: 'The poet thinks war is noble and worthwhile: he describes the soldiers as heroes and says that their glory will last a long time, even though they died. The repetition of the word honour, reinforces this point at the end of the poem.)

Further challenge

- Provide the children with examples of other poems from past SATs papers. Allow them to answer the related questions in groups. Encourage them to discuss answers fully and look closely at the questions worth two or three marks.

Reading test: Poetry

The Charge of the Light Brigade

1. What is the overall theme of the poem? ______________________ (1 mark)

2. What is happening in verse 1? ______________________

______________________ (2 marks)

3. How do we know the soldiers are charging downhill? ______________________

______________________ (1 mark)

4. "Theirs but to do and die" What does the poet mean?

____

______________________ (2 marks)

5. In the first three verses how does the poet build a sense of foreboding? Find three quotes from the text. ______________________

____

______________________ (3 marks)

6. What indications does the poet give that the soldiers fought bravely? Use the language from the poem to support your argument. ______________________

____

______________________ (2 marks)

7. In verse 4 how does the poet make us aware that the Light Brigade is at a disadvantage? ______________________

______________________ (2 marks)

8. What nationality is the other army? ______________________ (1 mark)

9. How many of the Light Brigade rode out of the "Valley of Death"?

______________________ (1 mark)

10. What is the author's opinion of war? Provide evidence from the text to support your opinion. (Continue on another sheet if necessary.) ______________________

______________________ (3 marks)

Writing test: Shorter task (Web page)

Objectives

Y6. T3. S4.
To secure control of complex sentences, understanding how clauses can be manipulated to achieve different effects.

Y6. T3. T22.
To select the appropriate style and form to suit a specific purpose and audience, drawing on knowledge of different non-fiction text types.

Administering the practice test

1. Explain to the children that this lesson will help them prepare for the shorter writing task in the Key Stage 2 English test. In this task, every word counts: they are given 20 minutes to plan and write two or three paragraphs for a specific purpose. This short piece of writing is for inclusion within a larger text. Therefore the children will not be required to consider formatting. Instead, they should concentrate on their writing skills: particular attention will be paid to vocabulary and sentence construction.

2. Provide the children with photocopiable page 103. Tell them to read it carefully, thinking about both the purpose of the text and the target audience. They should also decide on a suitable style of writing style. (Formal? Chatty?)

3. Encourage the children to highlight key words and phrases on the prompt as they read it. Remind them that they will have 20 minutes to write and this will include planning time. They should use note form for planning, plan in the same tense in which they will be writing and, consider all aspects of the writing, particularly the ending.

Mark scheme

Sentence structure, punctuation and text organisation		Composition and effect	
1 mark	Grammar is sound. Uses simple sentences, often subject + verb. Some connections between sentences (eg through pronoun 'it'). Full stops and capital letters usually accurate.	1 mark	A short series of statements about the topic, with some evaluation.
2 marks	Simple connectives, some sentences expanded with description through adverbs and adjectives. Present tense maintained. Full stops, capital letters, question marks, commas and exclamation marks used accurately.	2–3 marks	A persuasive piece of writing, with some awareness of audience and use of detail. Some subject-specific vocabulary used. Overall level of formality may be inconsistent.
3 marks	Sentences are varied through use of expanded noun phrases, adverbs and use of subordinate clauses. Connections through text show cause and effect.	4–5 marks	Details support the purpose (to persuade). An objective and authoritative viewpoint is established and maintained. The personal views of the writer may be included, but do not dominate.
4 marks	Varied use of connectives and variety of compound and complex sentences. Range of punctuation used, including brackets, semi-colons and dashes.	6–7 marks	Effort to persuade reader is clear, detail is selected for its purpose. The writer's viewpoint is consistent and formal.
		8 marks	Knowledge of audience informs choice and placing of content. Viewpoint is convincing and a range of stylistic features is used to inform audience.

Moving children on

- Following this test, set the children individual writing targets based on their area of lowest score. For example: to use commas to support divisions in complex sentences. Ensure that both children and parents know their targets. Encourage the children to give thought to them in all their written work - not just in English.

Writing test: Shorter task (Web page)

Eating More Fruit

The Healthy Schools Initiative is writing a leaflet about how primary schools encourage a healthy lifestyle. The organisation has already launched pages on physical education (PE), after-school recreation and healthier menus for school meals.

The Healthy Schools Initiative would like you to plan and write the page dedicated to encouraging children aged 7–11 years to eat fruit at morning break-time, rather than less healthy alternatives.

- Before you start, make some notes on words and phrases to describe:
  - healthy snacks and their benefits
  - unhealthy snacks and their effects.

- Use the lines in the box below for writing your section of the leaflet.

Eating more fruit

- You can ask your teacher for more paper if you need it.

Writing test: Longer task (School website)

Objectives

Y6. T3. S1.
To revise the language conventions and grammatical features of the different types of text.

Y6. T3. S3.
To revise formal styles of writing.

Y6. T3. T22.
To select the appropriate style and form to suit a specific purpose and audience, drawing on knowledge of different non-fiction text types.

Administering the practice test

1. On page 105 you will find two writing prompts. For this lesson, cover up the lower prompt ('A Letter to Your Teacher') with a blank sheet of paper. Photocopy the remaining prompt 'School Website' and the Mark scheme on page 107 (one of each per child).

2. Explain to the children that this lesson will prepare them for the 'Writing test: Longer task' in the Key Stage 2 English test. This is the task where the children are expected to plan and develop their writing over several ideas or concepts. Tell the children that particular attention will be paid to the structure and coherence of the piece, so planning is important. This is different to the 'Writing test: Shorter task', which focuses more closely on individual words and sentences. The children should aim to show off their writing skills to the best of their ability.

3. Distribute the writing prompt, 'School Website'. Also provide the children with lined paper for their planning and writing. Tell the children to read the prompt carefully, deciding on the purpose of the writing (explanation) and the target audience (internet users). They should also consider what style of writing will best suit the text. (Formal? Chatty?) Encourage the children to highlight key words and phrases as they read the prompt, for example: introduce, describe, and so on.

4. Explain to the children that they will have 45 minutes to write, including planning time. For their planning, the children should use note form and plan in the same tense in which they will be writing. Careful attention needs to be paid to planning the structure; encourage the children to think in particular of how they will begin and end the piece. Remind the children that no marks are available for illustrations, so they should simply indicate the need for an illustration rather than drawing it themselves.

5. Exactly 30 minutes after the children began writing, tell them that they have 15 minutes to finish their writing and check their work. After 45 minutes, tell the children to stop writing. Say that their practice test is now over and that they will assess their own work.

6. Ask the children to sit with a partner; distribute the Mark scheme on page 107. Tell the children to work collaboratively on one piece of writing at a time, assessing how many marks it achieves in the three assessment areas. The children should begin at the top of the grid and highlight those targets they have achieved. The last highlighted target in each column will indicate the numbers of marks to be awarded for each assessment area.

Moving children on

- Look at where the highlighting stops on the children's self assessment. Ask the children to select a target from those not highlighted, which they should try and achieve next time they write.

Writing test: Longer task

School Website

Your school is thinking about redesigning its website.
Your task is to provide for the headteacher an outline of the text for the new home page.
This is to include details about:

- the location and background of the school
- the curriculum taught in lessons
- the staff and their roles and responsibilities.

The school would also like you to provide links from this page that will describe other aspects of school life, such as after-school clubs, the school council and anything else you think is important.
As you plan, think about:

- the overall structure of the homepage
- how you will introduce the school
- how you will describe the location
- the words and phrases that you will use to describe the location, curriculum and staff at your school
- the other aspects of school life that you wish to cover.

Writing test: Longer task

A Letter to Your Teacher

Your teacher is thinking about setting extra English, maths and science homework for you over the school holidays. The pupils in your class are unhappy about this. Here are some of their views:
"This homework is extra to what we are normally given and I already struggle."
"I am busy in the holidays. When will I do the homework?"
"We are under enough pressure without being given more work to do."
"I am happy to have the extra work but I don't want other people to panic."
Your task is to write a letter to your teacher, expressing the views of the class and trying to persuade the teacher not to set the extra homework.
As you plan, think about:

- the overall format and structure of the letter: how will you begin and end it?
- the words and phrases that you will use to try to persuade your teacher not to set the extra homework
- anything else you think will be important, such as a possible solution to the problem.

Writing test: Longer task (Letter)

Objectives

Y5. T3. T17.
To draft and write individual, group or class letters for real purposes.

Y5. T3. T19.
To construct an argument in note form or full text to persuade others of a point of view.

Y6. T3. S1.
To revise the language conventions and grammatical features of the different types of text.

Administering the practice test

1. On page 105 you will find two writing prompts. For this lesson, cover up the upper prompt ('School Website') with a blank sheet of paper. Photocopy the remaining prompt 'A Letter to Your Teacher' and the Mark scheme on page 107 (one of each per child). This lesson, like the previous one, will help children prepare for the 'Writing test: Longer task' in the Key Stage 2 English test. This is the task where the children are expected to plan and develop their writing over several ideas or concepts. Remind the children of their previous writing targets. Ask: Which aspect of your writing did you need to improve? How could you have gained more marks on previous tests? Tell the children that in this second test they should aim to achieve higher marks than previously.

2. Distribute the writing prompt 'A Letter to Your Teacher', along with lined paper for planning and writing. Tell the children to read the prompt carefully, deciding on the purpose (persuasion) and the target audience (you/their teacher). They should also consider which style of writing will suit the text. (Formal? Chatty?) Encourage the children to highlight key words and phrases as they read: views of the class and persuade, for example.

3. Explain to the children that they will have 45 minutes to write, including planning time. For their planning, the children should use note form and plan in the same tense in which they will be writing. Careful attention should be paid to planning the structure; encourage the children to consider in particular how they will open and close the letter, what the contents of each paragraph will be and how they will ensure that the letter 'flows' from one paragraph to another.

4. Exactly 30 minutes after the children began writing, tell them that they have 15 minutes to finish their writing and check their work. After 45 minutes, tell the children to stop their work. Say that their practice test is now over and that they will assess their own work.

5. Provide the children with the Mark scheme on page 107 and ask them to independently assess their own work within the assessment areas given. Ask the children whether they have achieved their target from the previous writing session. Ask: Did you include connectives? Is your letter in paragraphs? Have you used a wide range of punctuation marks? Where children have achieved their target, encourage them to set new goals. Encourage all the children to compare their score (out of 28) with previous scores on similar tests. Ask: Who has made the most progress? What did we do differently today to ensure we would achieve a higher mark?

Moving children on

- Ask the children to edit their writing to fit a higher mark bracket. This may involve reordering sentences or adding adverbial phrases. Can the children develop further in the area of 'Text structure and organisation'? Ensure that they can plan accurately the structure of a variety of texts.

Writing test: Longer tasks (Mark scheme)

Sentence structure and punctuation		Text structure and organisation		Composition and effect	
1 mark	Most of my grammar is correct (my sentences make sense). I have used *and, but* and *then* to join clauses. Some of my sentences have capital letters and full stops.	1 mark	I have grouped my ideas into sequences of sentences on each topic. I have used simple connectives, eg *and, then.* I have used pronouns, eg *it, you, they.*	1–2 mark	I have written a short series of points about the school/homework. I have included basic details and simple statements, eg *The school is for children aged 4–11.* or *We are setting homework to do in the holidays.*
2–3 marks	I used simple connectives *and, but, then* and *because.* There are some adjectives, eg *nice, busy, big, small* in my work. I have used simple noun phrases, eg *The school is, Lessons are.* Full stops, capital letters, exclamation marks and question marks are used correctly. I have used commas in lists.	2–3 marks	I have given a brief introduction and conclusion, eg welcoming the reader to the school's web page. I have used words like *also* to add additional information. I have built up connections between my sentences using topic words, eg *teachers, marking, work.*	3–5 marks	I have explained about the school with some explanation of basic details, eg *St Mark's School is a primary school for children aged up to 11 years. Homework helps us to practise the work we started in school.* I have chosen to use relevant vocabulary, eg *educational, lessons, teachers,* etc. I have explained using facts alone, not my own opinion.
4–5 marks	I have used some complex sentences where I explain in more detail using connectives such as *if, because* and *when* (eg *if parents work*). I used the present tense in most sentences, eg *the school is...* I expressed possibilities using words such as *could* and *might.* Most of my sentences have accurate punctuation and I have used commas to separate clauses in complex sentences.	4–5 marks	My whole text is logically organised, including an introductory paragraph, ordered points and a conclusion. Within my paragraphs all points are linked to the first sentence. They develop or expand on one topic.	6–8 marks	I have tried to engage my audience by adding interesting facts, eg *There is a before-school facility for the children of working parents.* I have maintained a formal approach to the home page throughout. I have used generalisations, eg *Most staff run after school clubs. Most primary children receive homework.* I have used relevant educational, ICT or persuasive vocabulary.
6–7 marks	I have used a variety of sentences, including simple and complex sentences and questions. I use words like *which, until* and *where* to make longer sentences. I have some sentences written in the past tense and I also explore the future. I have used a range of punctuation, including brackets, dashes and colons.	6–7 marks	My overall text is in paragraphs. My paragraphs are all related to one another. Within each paragraph there is a full explanation of the main point. The conclusion links back to some items mentioned in previous paragraphs.	9–11 marks	I have written my whole text/letter formally, explaining the features of the school in a consistent way or outlining strongest arguments before weaker ones. I have used stylistic features to enhance my explanation, eg emotive vocabulary or rhetorical questions. I have maintained the style of a web page addressing an audience via the internet/a letter addressing my teacher.
8 marks	The length and structure of most of my sentences are different to focus on key ideas. I have made clever choices with my word order to emphasise my points.	8 marks	The whole of my text is well structured. The sequence of paragraphs adds to the overall effectiveness. I have presented the most important details first and less significant details later on. My individual paragraphs are structured differently.	12 marks	I have used stylistic features to make the home page/letter engaging, eg the inclusion of links to other pages, the ability to contact via email, the inclusion of a search engine etc or persuasive phrases which will appeal to the teacher (*Like you, we work hard during term time; we too need our rest.*)

This mark scheme relates to the two tasks appearing on page 105. Teacher's notes are provided on pages 104 and 106.

Photocard driving licences

Driver and Vehicle Licensing Agency (DVLA)

1. PHOTOCARD DRIVING LICENCES

DVLA now only issues photocard driving licences. This is to improve road safety by eliminating impersonation at driving tests and ensuring the person driving a vehicle is qualified to do so.

You will be issued with;

- a photocard; showing
  - the driver's photograph and signature which is electronically copied from the application form
  - categories of vehicles the driver is entitled to drive
- a paper counterpart document; showing
  - your signature (also electronically copied)
  - details of any endorsements, and in the case of a full licence holder, any provisional driving entitlement held.

Note: You must produce *both* the photocard and counterpart if requested by the police or a court. You should also present both parts when taking a driving test. You may also find that other organisations, such as car hire firms and insurance companies, will ask to see both parts.

Drivers will need to renew their photocard licence every ten years until age 70 to keep the photograph up-to-date. This will not affect the validity period of the entitlement shown on the licence. DVLA will send a reminder when the photograph is due for renewal. Drivers who are required to renew their licence at shorter intervals, for example, for medical reasons, or because they hold entitlement to drive buses or lorries, will not be required to renew their photograph at each renewal.

http://www.dvla.gov.uk/forms/pdf/D100.pdf

SCHOLASTIC

www.scholastic.co.uk

What is a visa?

If you are not a British Citizen or a citizen of one the European Economic Area (EEA) countries, you may need an entry clearance before you travel to the UK.

People from certain countries, known as visa nationals, need an entry clearance to enter the UK for any reason; those from other countries need one only for some reasons: for example, to live as the wife or husband of a British Citizen.

Entry clearance is the formal term to describe the application process for visa nationals who wish to travel to the United Kingdom and for non visa nationals who intend a longer stay or to settle in the UK. The entry clearance certificate, more commonly called a visa, is placed in your passport or travel document.

The job of an entry clearance officer at a British mission overseas is to decide if you qualify for entry before you travel to the United Kingdom. Entry clearance officers work to strict rules and procedures. Go to the **Immigration Rules** and **Diplomatic Service Procedures – Entry Clearance** for further information.

If you have a valid UK visa, you will not normally be refused entry to the UK on arrival unless your circumstances have changed, you gave false information, or you did not tell the entry clearance officer important facts when you applied for your visa.

The visa tells the immigration officer at a UK port of arrival:

- the purpose of your travel
- how long you can stay in the UK; and
- the latest date that you can enter the UK.

Normally, you may enter and leave the UK as many times as you like during the validity of your visa.

To find out if you need an entry clearance, go to: **Do I need a UK visa?**

http:www.ukvisas.gov.uk

Rama is banished

King Dashrati was fortunate. He ruled over a peaceful land and his three wives – Kausalya, Kaikeyi and Simitra – had all given him sons. But he knew he was getting old. "It would be good to retire now and let Rama take over the kingdom," he mused. So he ordered preparations to begin for Rama's coronation.

In the palace at Ayodhya, however, the youngest of King Dashrati's wives, Queen Kaikeyi, had nothing to do except think about herself. Her scheming maid, Manthara, saw her chance to put some mischief into Kaikeyi's head.

"Have you considered what might happen to you when Rama becomes king, mistress?" she asked Kaikeyi.

"What do you mean?" said Kaikeyi. "Rama loves me like his own mother."

"No doubt," purred Manthara. "But you are *not* his mother. You cannot expect to hold the same position of power that you had with King Dashrati."

Kaikeyi thought about it.

"What do you think I should do?" she asked Manthara.

"I think you should remind Dashrati of his promise to grant you two wishes, which he made to you when you saved his life. Remember?"

"Oh, yes," said Kaikeyi, doubtfully. "And then what?"

"You must ask him to put your son Bharata on the throne instead, and send Rama away."

That afternoon, Kaikeyi went into the anger room, where it was customary to get rid of angry feelings. She threw herself down, beating the floor in frustration. As she expected, King Dashrati came to her.

"My dear Kaikeyi," he said. "What troubles you?"

"You promised me two wishes," she said. "I want you to banish Rama for fourteen years and give the kingdom to Bharata instead."

The king was appalled. "How could you ask this of me, Kaikeyi?"

"You promised!" she repeated. "If you truly love me, you will grant my wishes!"

The king had no choice. Overnight his happiness had been destroyed. He could not face Rama and let Kaikeyi speak for him.

Rama listened to Kaikeyi and accepted his fate for the sake of his father. "I am sure Bharata will be a good king," he said. Accompanied by his wife Sita, and his faithful brother Lakshman, he went off into the forest to begin his banishment.

Jackie Andrews

The kidnapping of Sita

One day, Sita was picking flowers in the forest when a deer wandered across her path.

"Oh! What a beautiful creature!" cried Sita, and she ran back to the house to ask Rama to catch it for her.

Rama loved to give Sita everything she desired. Leaving her in the care of his brother, he set off to capture the deer. But as it led him deeper and deeper into the forest, Rama began to suspect that it was not a deer at all, but a demon in disguise, and he shot it with an arrow. As the creature died, it let out a terrible cry that sounded just like Rama.

Across the forest, Sita and Lakshman heard the cry.

"Rama is hurt! Please go and help him, Lakshman!" Sita begged.

"I must stay here and look after you!" he insisted. He was not at all sure that the voice was Rama's.

"Will you leave your brother to die?" demanded Sita, very upset.

Reluctantly, Lakshman agreed to go. He warned Sita to stay inside the house, which he had protected with a magic circle, then he ran off into the forest after Rama.

As soon as he had gone, the demon lord Ravana came to the house, disguised as a holy man. "Could you spare me some food, please?" he asked Sita.

Now every Hindu has a duty to give offerings to holy men, and Sita – forgetting Lakshman's warning – fetched a bowl of fruit for her visitor.

The moment Sita stepped outside the protection of the house, Ravana turned back into his own monstrous shape. He snatched up Sita and flew off with her in his terrible chariot that was drawn by a thousand mules with the heads of goblins. Across the skies they swept, southwards towards Lanka.

Jackie Andrews

Night-time encounter from *The BFG*

In the moonlight, Sophie caught a glimpse of an enormous long pale wrinkly face with the most enormous ears. The nose was as sharp as a knife, and above the nose there were two bright flashing eyes, and the eyes were staring straight at Sophie. There was a fierce and devilish look about them.

Sophie gave a yelp and pulled back from the window. She flew across the dormitory and jumped into her bed and hid under the blanket.

And there she crouched, still as a mouse, and tingling all over...

The Snatch

Under the blanket, Sophie waited.

After a minute or so, she lifted a corner of the blanket and peeped out.

For the second time that night her blood froze to ice and she wanted to scream, but no sound came out. There at the window, with the curtains pushed aside, was the enormous long pale wrinkly face of the Giant Person, staring in. The flashing black eyes were fixed on Sophie's bed.

The next moment, a huge hand with pale fingers came snaking in through the window. This was followed by an arm, an arm as thick as a tree-trunk, and the arm, the hand, the fingers were reaching out across the room towards Sophie's bed.

This time Sophie really did scream, but only for a second because very quickly the huge hand clamped down over her blanket and the scream was smothered by the bedclothes.

Sophie, crouching underneath the blanket, felt strong fingers grasping hold of her, and then she was lifted up from her bed, blanket and all, and whisked out of the window.

Roald Dahl

Blackout

Lewisham, London
Friday 2 Aug 1940

The strangest thing happened yesterday, really frightening. It's getting dark slightly earlier again now, and when I went up to bed at about nine o'clock there wasn't enough light to read. Shirl needed to take off her warpaint and we had two candles lit in the room so we could both just about see without having the electric on. Anyway, we mustn't have drawn the curtains properly, because five minutes later there's a huge knock on the door like the world's coming to an end and when Mum answers she finds a policeman on the doorstep making a fuss. Then he elbows his way past her into the house, saying someone's signalling to the Germans.

Mum tells him as politely as she can that he must be off his rocker, but he demands to see our room and waltzes upstairs to give us a right bawling out, shouting didn't we know there was a blackout and were we on Jerry's side? Shirl was completely shocked and embarrassed, and I cowered under the eiderdown. Good job Shirl still had most of her clothes on!

When he'd finally gone Mum went completely mad. She didn't know whether to be more annoyed with us for showing her up, or with him for being so rude and barging in like that. Shirl and I ended up in tears and all in all it was a horrible end to the evening. When Dad came home at the end of his shift this morning, Mum packed him off down the police station to tell the desk sergeant what he thought, but I don't see what good that'll do.

I suppose the blackout's necessary. It makes sense that we shouldn't give the Jerry bombers any idea of what's on the ground, but it doesn't half cause problems. Dad said it was a good thing it was only a beat copper and not one of the ARP wardens who usually go round telling people to put lights out, because they really *are* little dictators. Then Mum shocked us all by saying that if you can't beat 'em you should join 'em, and that she thought she'd apply to be a warden, because none of them had two grains of sense to rub together and if things got really nasty we couldn't afford to leave it to morons.

Vince Cross

AIR RAID

I woke up when the bomb came through the roof. It came through at an angle, overflew my bed by inches, bounced over my mother's bed, hit the mirror, dropped into the grate and exploded up the chimney. It was an incendiary. A fire-bomb.

My brother Ivan appeared in pyjamas and his Home Guard tin hat. Being in the Home Guard, he had ensured that all the rooms in our house were stuffed with sandbags. Ivan threw sand over the bomb but the dry sand kept sliding off. He threw the hearthrug over the bomb and jumped up and down on it, until brother Pud arrived with a bucket of wet sand from the yard. This did the trick.

Mother grabbed me from the bed. The night sky was filled with lights. Searchlights, anti-aircraft fire, stars and a bombers' moon. The sky bounced as my mother ran. Just as we reached our dug-out across the street, the sky flared red as the church exploded.

It was Monday, 21 April 1941, just before 10pm. Thousands of incendiaries were dropped on our village, Pakefield, and the neighbouring big town, Lowestoft. The Germans were trying to set alight the thatched roof of the church to make a beacon for the following waves of bombers. Within a few minutes more than forty fires were blazing in Pakefield and the southern part of Lowestoft. Two incendiaries buried themselves in the roof of the church. The Rector climbed the ladders to extinguish one, but was unable to reach the other.

The high-explosive bombs followed immediately. More were dropped in this raid than in any other, but with the church now blazing, a thick mist rolled up from the sea and ruined the bombers' night. The following waves of bombers turned back.

Michael Foreman

From *War Boy* by Michael Foreman (1989, Pavilion)

It's mould magic

IT ALL BEGAN about 14 years ago, at St Mary's Hospital in London. I've never been very tidy, and my laboratory was piled high with glass dishes containing old samples of bacteria.

For many years, I had been hunting for a new kind of medicine – one that could be swallowed, to kill dangerous bacteria inside the body. But after years of work, I'd yet to make a breakthrough.

Well, the dirty dishes were in the sink, ready to be washed. I was about to disinfect them, when I saw a bluish-grey mould growing on one of them. Then I looked closer and noticed something peculiar. The bacteria all around the edges of the mould had died. When I saw that, I forgot the washing up in a flash!

MOULD MYSTERY

Could it have been the mould that had killed the germs? I quickly took a sample of mould and tested it. With growing astonishment, I found it contained a chemical that killed many kinds of bacteria – including the ones that cause deadly diseases like scarlet fever, diphtheria and pneumonia.

The mould is actually very widespread – you've probably seen it growing on rotten fruit! Its name is ***Penicillium notatum****, so I called this remarkable chemical "penicillin".*

However, the mould juice itself only produced very small quantities of penicillin – not nearly enough to work inside the body. And to make enough for medicine would be a difficult task.

I had other pressing work at the time, and I was forced to leave the development of penicillin to others. So it wasn't until 1938 that Howard Florey and Ernst Chain – two brilliant scientists at Oxford – got to work on penicillin.

INCREDIBLE CURE

After two years, enough pure penicillin had been extracted from the mould for it to be tested on some diseased mice. The results were amazing. Mice given a dose of the drug were fit and well a few hours later, while those without it died.

Then came the final test. Penicillin was given to human patients – to dying people who had no other hope left. And it cured them!

In the future, penicillin will save millions. Not bad for something that began with a single dirty dish!

Phil Gates

The brain

THE HUMAN BRAIN fills the top half of the head. It is soft in texture and weighs about 1.4kg (3lbs). From the outside, the brain is divided into two halves, called hemispheres. Each hemisphere is covered by a layer of the brain called the cerebrum. The surface of the cerebrum is heavily wrinkled. This allows more brain cells to be packed into the restricted space inside your head. To the rear of the brain, and tucked in just under the cerebrum, is another part of the brain called the cerebellum. Projecting out from just in front of the cerebellum is the long, thin spinal cord that runs down your spine.

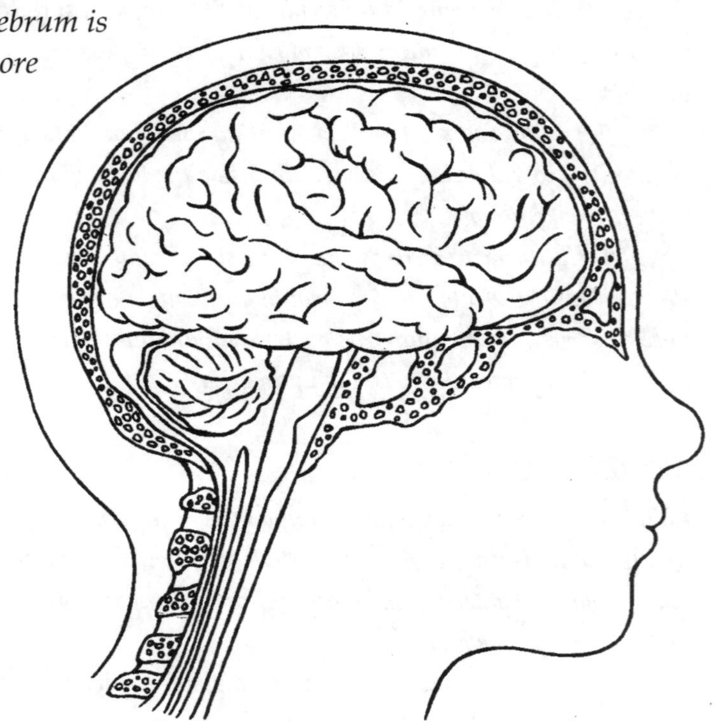

BLOOD TO THE BRAIN

Even though the brain weighs one-fiftieth of your body weight, it still receives one-fifth of your blood supply, bringing nutrients to fuel its activity. Delivering this blood is a network of tiny blood vessels that runs between the skull and the brain.

Each half of the cerebrum, which covers the surface of the brain, is divided into four parts, called lobes. These are the frontal lobe under the forehead, the parietal lobe on the top of the brain, the temporal lobe on the side of the brain and the occipital lobe on the back of the brain. Inside the brain lie the parts that are involved with your emotions and the automatic running of your body.

If a small part of one of the arteries supplying blood to the brain expands it can cut off the blood supply to the brain. It can also cause blood to leak out into the layer surrounding the brain. This is called an aneurysm. The leaked blood can put great pressure on the brain and if this pressure is not released in time it can cause a stroke. Damage can also be caused by a blocked blood vessel, called a thrombosis.

Steve Parker

From *Look at your body – Brain and Nerves* by Steve Parker (1998, Franklin Watts)

SCHOLASTIC
www.scholastic.co.uk

PHOTOCOPIABLE

THE SUN

Solar surface

The Sun makes sunlight by burning four million tonnes (tons) of fuel every second. You can see in this picture that the Sun's surface is a churning mass of explosions. Solar flares and fiery loops of gas leap out into space.

This is a solar prominence. It is a massive arch of hot gas, which reaches out into space like a huge, flaming tongue.

The Sun is a star. It is a huge ball of blazing gas that makes vast amounts of light and heat which we call sunshine. It is so big it could hold a million planets the size of Earth. It looks like it's burning, but it's actually exploding like a massive bomb.

The solar wind

As well as light and heat, the Sun also sends out a stream of invisible specks, called particles, into space. This is called the solar wind. When the particles pass by the North and South Poles of Earth they can make the air glow beautiful reds, blues, greens and purples.

The Sun's surface is called the photosphere. The temperature there is 5,500°C (10,000°F). The dark areas are sunspots. The temperature is lower there.

Sometimes white areas appear on the surface of the Sun. These are called faculae. The temperature here is even higher than that of the rest of the Sun.

Liquid, ice or gas?

Life exists on Earth because our planet is just the right distance from the Sun for water to be liquid, rather than ice or a gas.

Sun

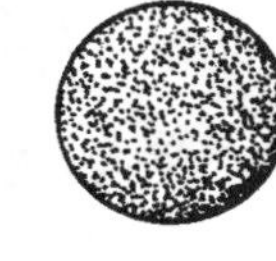

Mars is too cold.

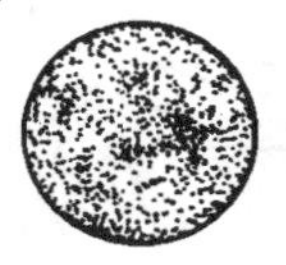

Venus is too hot.

Earth is just right.

From *The Usborne Little Encyclopedia of Space* (2001, Usborne Publishing)

How you breathe

Every time you breathe, you move air in and out of your lungs. This makes sure that life-giving oxygen gets to the lungs, while waste carbon dioxide is removed. But your lungs cannot move on their own. Breathing depends on your ribs and diaphragm, a sheet of muscle under the lungs. They make your lungs suck in and squeeze out air through your nose and mouth.

Oxygen from the air passes from the lungs into the blood. The blood then carries oxygen to the body's cells, picks up waste carbon dioxide, and carries this back to the lungs where it is breathed out.

To breathe in, the muscles between your ribs pull the ribs up and out, and your diaphragm pushes down. This makes more space in your chest, and air is sucked into your lungs. When you breathe out, your rib muscles move down, and your diaphragm moves up. The space in your chest reduces, and air is squeezed from your lungs.

Breathing in

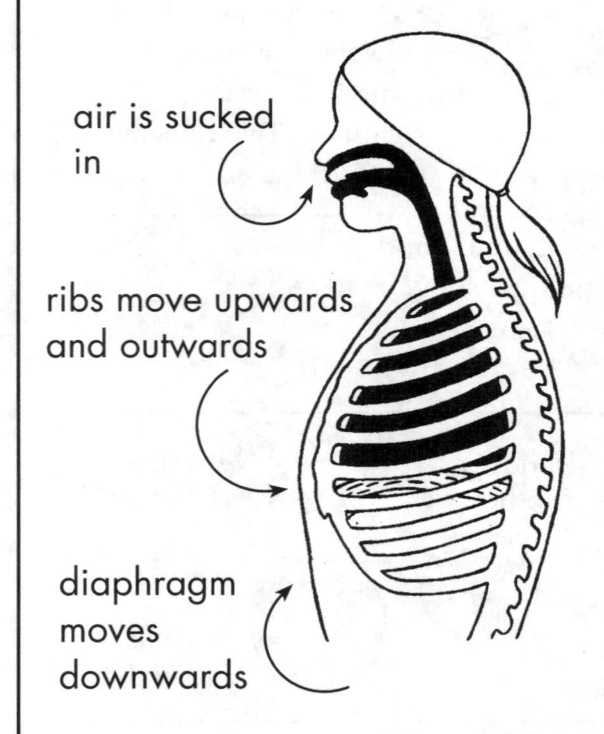

Breathing out

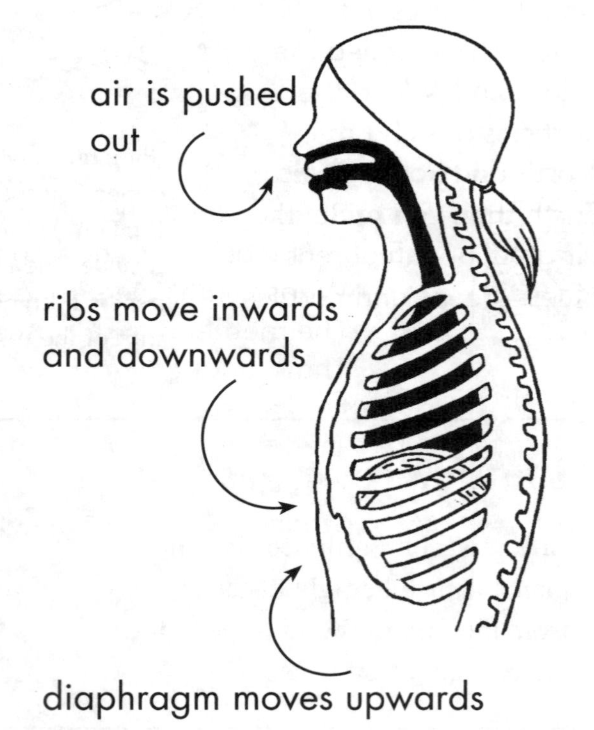

King Henry V

Act III, Scene 1

Alarum. Enter the King followed by soldiers

1 Once more unto the breach, dear friends, once more;
Or close the wall up with our English dead.
In peace there's nothing so becomes a man
As modest stillness and humility:
5 But when the blast of war blows in our ears,
Then imitate the action of the tiger;
Stiffen the sinews, summon up the blood,
Disguise fair nature with hard-favour'd rage;
Then lend the eye a terrible aspect;
10 Let pry through the portage of the head
Like the brass cannon; let the brow o'erwhelm it
As fearfully as doth a galled rock
O'erhang and jutty his confounded base,
Swill'd with the wild and wasteful ocean.
15 Now set the teeth and stretch the nostril wide,
Hold hard the breath and bend up every spirit
To his full height. On, on, you noblest English.
Whose blood is fet from fathers of war-proof!
Fathers that, like so many Alexanders,
20 Have in these parts from morn till even fought
And sheathed their swords for lack of argument:
Dishonour not your mothers; now attest
That those whom you call'd fathers did beget you.
Be copy now to men of grosser blood,
25 And teach them how to war. And you, good yeomen,
Whose limbs were made in England, show us here
The mettle of your pasture; let us swear
That you are worth your breeding; which I doubt not;
For there is none of you so mean and base,
30 That hath not noble lustre in your eyes.
I see you stand like greyhounds in the slips,
Straining upon the start. The game's afoot:
Follow your spirit, and upon this charge
Cry "God for Harry, England, and Saint George!"

Exeunt. Alarum, and chambers go off

William Shakespeare

The Mad Hatter's tea party

There was a table set out under a tree in front of the house, and the March Hare and the Hatter were having tea at it: a Dormouse was sitting between them, fast asleep, and the other two were resting their elbows on it, and talking over its head. "Very uncomfortable for the Dormouse," thought Alice; "only, as it's asleep, I suppose it doesn't mind."

The table was a large one, but the three were all crowded together at one corner of it: "No room! No room!" they cried out when they saw Alice coming. "There's *plenty* of room!" said Alice indignantly, and she sat down in a large arm-chair at one end of the table.

"Have some wine," the March Hare said in an encouraging tone.

Alice looked all around the table, but there was nothing on it but tea. "I don't see any wine," she remarked.

"There isn't any," said the March Hare.

"Then it wasn't very civil of you to offer it," said Alice angrily.

"It wasn't very civil of you to sit down without being invited," said the March Hare.

"I didn't know it was *your* table" said Alice; "it's laid for a great many more than three."

"Your hair wants cutting" said the Hatter. He had been looking at Alice for some time with great curiosity, and this was his first speech.

"You shouldn't make personal remarks," Alice said with some severity; "it's very rude."

The Hatter opened his eyes very wide on hearing this; but all he *said* was, "Why is a raven like a writing-desk?"

"Come, we shall have some fun now!" thought Alice. "I'm glad they've begun asking riddles. – I believe I can guess that," she added aloud.

"Do you mean that you think you can find out the answer to it?" said the March Hare.

"Exactly so," said Alice.

"Then you should say what you mean," the March Hare went on.

"I do," Alice hastily replied ; "at least – at least I mean what I say – that's the same thing, you know."

"Not the same thing a bit!" said the Hatter. "You might just as well say that 'I see what I eat' is the same thing as 'I eat what I see'!"

Lewis Carroll

Limerick

There was a Young Lady whose Nose
Continually prospers and grows;
When it grew out of sight,
She exclaimed in a fright,
"Oh! Farewell to the end of my Nose!"

Edward Lear

On the Ning Nang Nong

On the Ning Nang Nong
Where the Cows go Bong!
And the Monkeys all say Boo!
There's a Nong Nang Ning
Where the trees go Ping!
And the teapots Jibber Jabber Joo.
On the Nong Ning Nang
All the mice go Clang!
And you just can't catch 'em when they do!
So it's Ning Nang Nong!
Cows go Bong!
Nong Nang Ning!
Trees go Ping!
Nong Ning Nang!
The mice go Clang!
What a noisy place to belong,
Is the Ning Nang Ning Nang Nong!!

Spike Milligan

The Mad Hatter's Song

Twinkle, twinkle, little bat!
How I wonder what you're at!
Up above the world you fly,
Like a tea tray in the sky.
Twinkle, twinkle —

Lewis Carroll

Dulce et Decorum Est

Bent double, like old beggars under sacks,
Knock-kneed, coughing like hags, we cursed through sludge,
Till on the haunting flares we turned our backs
And towards our distant rest began to trudge.
Men marched asleep. Many had lost their boots
But limped on, blood-shod. All went lame; all blind;
Drunk with fatigue; deaf even to the hoots
Of tired, outstripped Five-Nines that dropped behind.

Gas! Gas! Quick, boys! – An ecstasy of fumbling,
Fitting the clumsy helmets just in time;
But someone still was yelling out and stumbling,
And flound'ring like a man on fire or lime...
Dim, through the misty panes and thick green light,
As under a green sea, I saw him drowning.
In all my dreams, before my helpless sight,
He plunges at me, guttering, choking, drowning.

If in some smothering dreams you too could pace
Behind the wagon that we flung him in,
And watch the white eyes writhing in his face,
His hanging face, like a devil's sick of sin;
If you could hear, at every jolt, the blood
Come gargling from the froth-corrupted lungs,
Obscene as cancer, bitter as the cud
Of vile, incurable sores on innocent tongues, –
My friend, you would not tell with such high zest
To children ardent for some desperate glory,
The old Lie: Dulce et decorum est
Pro patria mori.

Wilfred Owen

The Soldier

If I should die, think only this of me:
That there's some corner of a foreign field
That is forever England. There shall be
In that rich earth a richer dust concealed;
A dust whom England bore, shaped, made aware,
Gave, once, her flowers to love, her ways to roam,
A body of England's, breathing English air,
Washed by the rivers, blest by suns of home.

And think, this heart, all evil shed away,
A pulse in the eternal mind, no less
Gives somewhere back the thoughts by England given;
Her sights and sounds; dreams happy as her day;
And laughter, learnt of friends; and gentleness,
In hearts at peace, under an English heaven.

Rupert Brooke

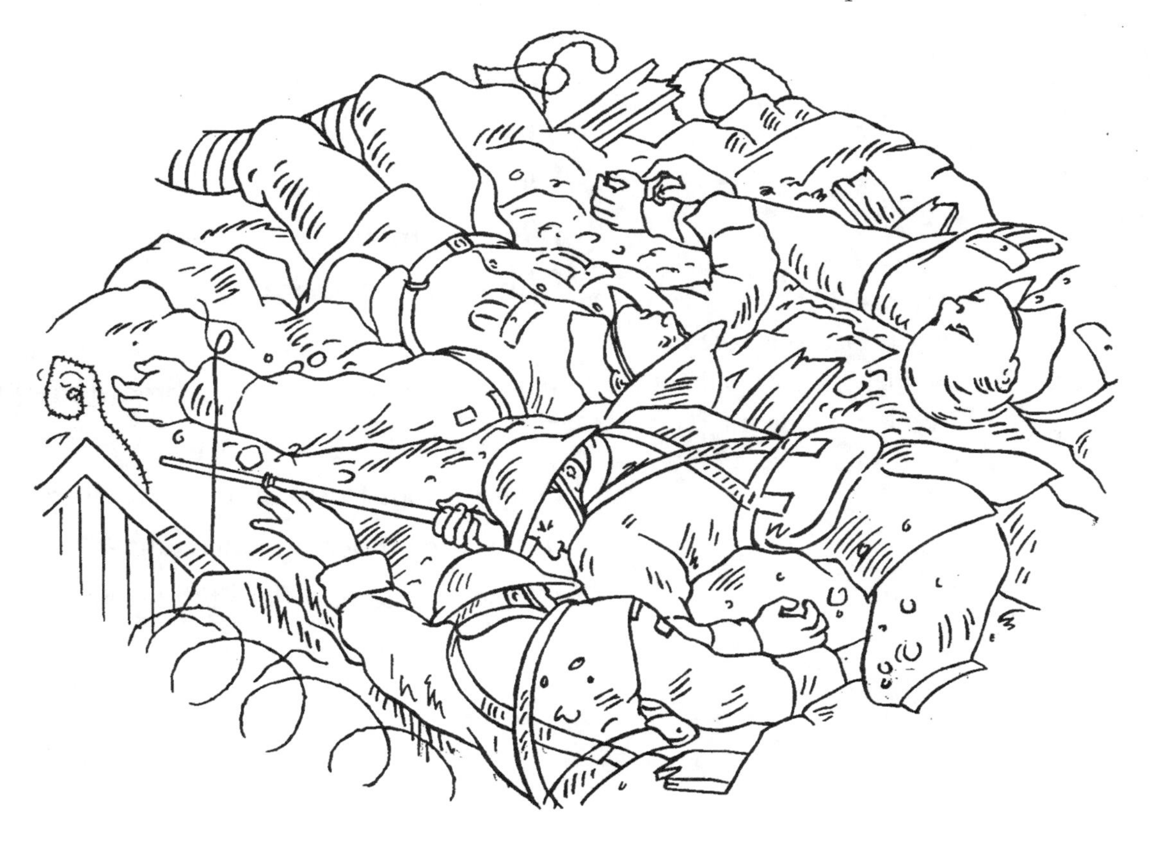

Simple Seasons

Swallows
Primroses
Return.
It's
New,
Green!

Skylarks
Up,
Meadows
Motley,
Elms
Regal.

Apples
Untold,
Trees
Unruly;
Mists
Now.

Waters
Icebound,
Naked
Trees;
Earth
Rests.

Eric Finney

Seasons

Springtime casts a spell of green,
Paints flowers opening to the sun.
Rain falls softly, saying "Wake",
In a fresh world just begun.
New leaves and buds, birds and lambs,
Grow and burst, hatch and run.

Summer, when we lie on grass
Under shimmer of blue sky.
Murmuring bees, shade of trees,
Matching butterflies flutter by.
Evening holds the scent of flowers,
Racing in lightness, swallows fly.

Autumn, when the leaves turn red,
Umber and amber and then fly.
The wispy smoke of bonfires drifts
Upwards in the evening sky.
Morning mists blur scarlet berries,
Nuts and apples drop and lie.

Winter, when your warm breath smokes
In the bitter morning chill.
Night brings frosts that creep and crisp.
Trees are stretching black and still,
Etching patterns where the bright
Robin makes a whistling trill.

Jo Peters

Reasons for Seasons

In the spring Jialu loves playing
When the flowers start to bloom,
In the park and in the playground,
In the kitchen and her room.
She talks to passing butterflies
And if a bird's in song,
She knows just how to harmonise
And so she sings along.

In the summer Jialu loves playing—
She loves summer a lot.
She plays tennis and goes swimming
When the sun shines very hot.
She runs up hills, she runs down hills,
Sometimes she runs round and round.
When she gets too hot she eats jelly—
It helps to cool her down!

In the autumn Jialu loves playing
As the leaves begin to fall.
When smart squirrels start to store food
She's out playing with her ball.
When the days start to get shorter
And the weather's not so kind,
Jialu finds it hard to keep still—
She's got good times on her mind.

In the winter when it's freezing
And there's bright white snow and ice,
Jialu simply starts believing
That the weather's very nice.
She thinks the seasons are amazing,
She plays each day of the year.
She thinks life is meant for playing,
She thinks that is why she's here.

Benjamin Zephaniah

The Fight of the Year

"And there goes the bell for the third month
and Winter comes out of his corner looking groggy
Spring leads with a left to the head
followed by a sharp right to the body
daffodils
primroses
crocuses
snowdrops
lilacs
violets
pussywillow
Winter can't take much more punishment
and Spring shows no sign of tiring
tadpoles
squirrels
baalambs
badgers
bunny rabbits
mad march hares
horses and hounds
Spring is merciless
Winter won't go the whole twelve rounds
bobtail clouds
scallywaggy winds
the sun
the pavement artist
in every town
A left to the chin
and Winter's down!
1 tomatoes
2 radish
3 cucumber
4 onions
5 beetroot
6 celery
7 and any
8 amount
9 of lettuce
10 for dinner
Winter is out for the count
Spring is the winner!"

Roger McGough

Room For One More

How difficult it was to sleep in that strange bed! She wrestled with the duvet and thumped the pillow; she turned her back on the flimsy curtains; she wished she had never come up to London.

At midnight she heard the grandfather clock whirr and strike; and then she heard the gravel in the driveway crunch. At once she jumped out of bed and crossed the room and just peeped between the curtains.

What she could see was a gleaming black hearse. But there was no coffin in it, and no flowers. No, the hearse was packed out with living people: a crush of talking, laughing, living people.

Then the driver of the hearse looked straight up at her, as she peeped between the curtains.

"There's room for one more." That's what he said. She could hear his voice quite clearly. Then she tugged the curtains so they crossed over, and ran back across the room, and jumped into bed, and pulled the duvet up over her head. And when she woke up the next morning, she really wasn't sure whether it was all a dream or not.

That day, she went shopping. In the big store, she did Levis Jeanswear on the fifth floor; she did Adidas Sportswear and that was on the sixth floor; and then she did cosmetics and that was on the seventh floor. Carrying two bags in each hand, she walked over to the lift. But when the bell pinged and the doors opened, she saw the lift was already jammed full with people.

The lift attendant looked straight at her as she stood there with her bags. "There's room for one more," he said. And his face was the face of the driver of the hearse.

"No," she said quickly. "No, I'll walk down."

Then the lift door closed with a clang. At once there was a kind of grating screech, and a terrible rattling, then a huge double thud.

The lift in the big store dropped from top to bottom of the shaft, and every single person in it was killed.

Kevin Crossley-Holland

Welsh Star Ready to Shine

Gavin Henson has been called the David Beckham of rugby union with good reason – he has what it takes.

He was one of the stars of the Wales side that won the Six Nations Championship last year. He is also a key player for the Ospreys, his club that took the Celtic League title last season. And Welsh singer Charlotte Church is his girlfriend.

So it was no surprise that he made many of the headlines on the recent British and Irish Lions bruising tour of New Zealand.

But it was not always for the right reasons. To almost everyone's surprise, coach Sir Clive Woodward left the 23-year-old out of the combined team of English, Scottish, Welsh and Irish players for the first Test in Christchurch.

Second choice

Woodward has since shocked the rugby world by taking a new job with Southampton Football Club, but he was criticised for his decision not to pick Henson as inside centre. Instead he picked many of the England players he had coached to the 2003 Rugby World Cup. Henson admitted that it was a massive disappointment not to be picked.

Henson broke back into the side for the second Test but injured his arm and missed the third match. It was a disappointing tour for the Lions who lost all three Tests by wide margins.

"I expected to play in Christchurch, it was a real shock not to," said Henson. "Sir Clive discussed it with me. He said he wanted to go with experience and with players he knew. I could understand his point and had a game a few days later.

"I was delighted to start the second Test, that crowned a great season for me. Lions tours are great things, the mixture of players and coaches from four countries is something unique. If I'm still playing well I hope to be with them when they next play in South Africa in 2009."

Title defence

Henson is now concentrating on helping the Ospreys make a good start to the season in the Celtic League when he and the other Welsh Lions players return to action in October. The Ospreys are defending their title. Henson also will play a key role as Wales chase another Six Nations title in the autumn.

The Welsh won the Grand Slam last year, beating England, Scotland, Ireland, France and Italy. This was an amazing turnaround as two years before they failed to win a match in the championship.

They play New Zealand on November 5 at the Millennium Stadium and after those tough friendly matches they will aim for a second Six Nations triumph in a row.

Welsh record

Henson was named the 2001 International Rugby Board Young Player of the Year after making his debut in the Wales No10 shirt when he was just 19 years old.

He switched positions a few times, to fly-half, centre and wing, but he is settled in his position now and last autumn he kicked a Welsh record, 14 conversion kicks out of 14 attempts against Japan.

From www.thenewspaper.org.uk

The Charge of the Light Brigade

Half a league, half a league,
Half a league onward,
All in the valley of Death
  Rode the six hundred.
"Forward, the Light Brigade!
Charge for the guns!" he said:
Into the valley of Death
  Rode the six hundred.

"Forward, the Light Brigade!"
Was there a man dismayed?
Not though the soldier knew
  Some one had blundered:
Theirs not to make reply,
Theirs not to reason why,
Theirs but to do and die:
Into the valley of Death
  Rode the six hundred.

Cannon to right of them,
Cannon to left of them,
Cannon in front of them
  Volleyed and thundered;
Stormed at with shot and shell,
Boldly they rode and well,
Into the jaws of Death,
Into the mouth of Hell
  Rode the six hundred.

Flashed all their sabres bare,
Flashed as they turned in air
Sabring the gunners there,
Charging an army, while
  All the world wondered:
Plunged in the battery-smoke
Right through the line they broke;
Cossack and Russian
Reeled from the sabre-stroke
  Shattered and sundered.
Then they rode back, but not,
  Not the six hundred.

Cannon to right of them,
Cannon to left of them,
Cannon behind them
  Volleyed and thundered;
Stormed at with shot and shell,
While horse and hero fell,
They that had fought so well
Came through the jaws of Death
Back from the mouth of Hell,
All that was left of them,
  Left of six hundred.

When can their glory fade?
O the wild charge they made!
  All the world wondered.
Honour the charge they made!
Honour the Light Brigade,
  Noble six hundred!

Alfred, Lord Tennyson